AN EXAMINATION OF THE MYSTIC TENDENCIES IN ISLÁM

other recent reference works from cosmo publications . . .

International Encyclopaedia of Islamic History
in 12 Volumes
Houtsma, M. Th., *et. al.*

International Encyclopaedia of Great Islamic Dynasties
in 4 Volumes
Houtsma, M. Th., *et. al.*

REDISCOVERING ISLAM
Encyclopaedia of Islamic Studies
in 35 Volumes
By Several Leading Islamic Scholars

Biographical Encyclopaedia of Islam
in 4 Volumes
Houtsma, M. Th; Wensink, A.J.; Arnold, T.W.; Heffering, W. & Levi-Provencal, E. *R*

Encyclopaedia of Islamic Mysticism and Sufism
in 23 Volumes

THE MUSLIMS
Encyclopaedia of Islam
in 11 Volumes
Ed. Subodh Kapoor

AN EXAMINATION OF THE MYSTIC TENDENCIES IN ISLÁM

IN THE LIGHT OF

THE QUR'ÁN AND TRADITIONS

By

M. M. ZUHURU'D-DIN AHMAD, MA., LL.B.,

Professor of Logic and Philosophy at the
Ismail College, Andheri (Bombay)
Teacher Post-graduates Classes at the Bombay University.
Sometime University Lecturer at Muslim University,
Aligarh, and at Islamia College, Calcutta.

Cosmo Publications

2012 INDIA

AN EXAMINATION OF THE
MYSTIC TENDENCIES IN ISLÁM

Published by
Cosmo Publications, 2012

ISBN 978-81-307-1190-4

Published by
COSMO PUBLICATIONS
for
GENESIS PUBLISHING PVT. LTD.
24-B, Ansari Road, Darya Ganj,
New Delhi-110 002,
INDIA

Printed and Bound in India

Dedicated

TO

Mr. AHMADBHOY FAZALBHOY KARIMBHOY,

B.A. (CANTAB.), BAR-AT-LAW

a scholar and patron of scholarship,

in token

of

his generous help,

without which the book could not have
been published.

PREFACE.

The aim of this book is to explain how mysticism originated and developed in the Islāmic world. The author has made an attempt to analyse the chief elements of the so-called Islāmic mysticism and to show in what way its basic principles are related to the fundamental tenets of Islām. It was necessary for this purpose to give a brief account of the founder of Islām and his companions, and to show how their life could have helped to suggest and develop the chief mystic theories among the Muslims. It is purported to be a criticism of the origin and development of the Sufi movement among the Muslims, in the light of the Qur'ān and Traditions of the prophet, the two chief sources of knowledge about Islām.

Western orientalists have been writing voluminous books with regard to the development of Mystic theories in the Islāmic world. But very often their efforts are marred by their reliance on the works of unknown authors. Their inferences from such works give an impression to the readers that the Muslim Mystics had lived a life absolutely different from the life and tenets of the founder of Islām. Their writings seem to suggest that Muslim saints had chalked out for themselves a path of spiritual progress, which had very little in common with the path of the prophet and his companions, and almost invariably aim at proving that this new path founded by these saints in some way made amends for the inherent defects of Islām as a theory of life. There is nothing farther from the truth than this suggestion of the Western scholars. The present writer has made an humble attempt to prove that the Muslim saints, the original founders of the different Sufi sects, were pious Muslims trying to follow the path of the prophet like the rest of believers, differing only in this respect that they were distinguished for their sincerity, piety, love and fear of God and their zeal in following the prophet in every detail of conduct. The later accretions to the Sufi theories were partly due to the peculiar conditions of the disintegrating and degenerating Islāmic society and partly due to the foreign influences which in the end deprived the Islāmic faith of its pristine purity. Various movements started in the Islāmic world with a view to purging Islāmic society of foreign elements have also been briefly described in the end.

The author has tried to rely on well known Sufi writers and has as far as possible avoided reference to books of doubtful authority. The works consulted are given in the footnotes in their respective places.

My thanks are due to Dr. Sir Radhakrishna, at present the Vice-Chancellor of Andhra University, who went through the manuscript when he was Chairman of the Post-Graduates Studies at Calcutta. My special thanks, however, are due to my esteemed friend Dr. U. M. Daudpota, M.A., Ph.D. (Cantab.), Professor of Arabic at the Ismail College, for reading the manuscript, for correcting the proofs and for directing me with regard to the treatment of the subject. But for his scholarly help, which he gave at the expense of his most valuable time, the book could not have been what it is now. In the end, I must also express my deep debt of gratitude to my master, the late Kāḍī Muḥammad Sulaimān of Mansūrpur, the author of Raḥmatu^{n}-l'il-'Ālamīn, and various other works of high literary quality, to whose teachings I owe much of my insight into the Qur'ān.

CONTENTS

PAGES

Mystic Tendencies in Islām

CHAPTER I.

INTRODUCTION.

There has already grown up an appreciable amount of literature dealing with the origin and development of mysticism in Islām. Efforts have been made to trace the various influences which gave rise to the doctrines of Sufism, but to a Muslim scholar of Islāmic literature these efforts appear only as so much labour wasted. It has almost become a fashion with writers to lay too much stress upon the external circumstances and to neglect the independent development of the Sufi doctrines which took place side by side with the development of theological, ontological, social, moral, and logical theories in the Islāmic world.

Sufism has passed through many stages each of which was more or less a resultant of the various influences which were working in the Islāmic world at that particular time. It was not the case with

Sufism alone, since almost every doctrine of Islām underwent some kind of change due to the similar influences. As Islām spread, it came in contact with religions, customs, myths and traditions, held by their adherents with as much sincerity, if not with equal fervour. The natural result of this intermingling of various civilisations and religious beliefs was mutual modification. But in all such modifications the Muslim principles preponderated, and there is not one instance in which the Muslims allowed any fundamental or basic principle of their faith to be compromised. In most cases the conquered not only adopted the faith of their conquerors but also their language—an occurrence which is unique in the history of the world. The Muslims, however, were not blind fanatics, and, therefore, whenever they came in contact with an ancient civilisation, with an heritage of learning and accumulated wisdom, they took full advantage of it and allowed themselves to be influenced by it.

The war between the Muslims and non-Muslims was a war of ideals, as every war more or less is, and whenever such a war occurred the dying and degenerate civilisation had to go down before the superior ideals of life preached by Islām.

The founder of Islām had given an interpretation of life which, in a way, was much loftier than ever ventured by any one before him. His teachings had infused a new life into all who had rallied round him, giving them an entirely new outlook on the problems of life and death, of good and evil, and of relations between the Creator and the creatures. Inspired by this new light, his followers were no less anxious to promulgate the new message to the others who had not yet joined their ranks. It was an interpretation of life in the light of certain ideals. Its aim was to teach the worth, the use, and the value of living for certain well defined ideals and objects, and according to certain principles, rather than giving a few casual and disconnected moral and philosophic wise sayings, at which the teachings of most of the other religions had stopped short. To take an instance, God enjoins His prophet in the Qur'ān to announce, "Say: my prayer, my sacrifice, my life and my death are for the sake of Allāh, the Lord of the worlds."[1] The ideal was thus given a paramount place in life, in comparison to which life and death were considered quite insignificant. In this way God, Love of God, Fear of God, and complete obedience to Him formed the essence of Islām, and constituted the most central principles of the teachings of its founder. He claimed to have been sent on this earth with the mission of propagating the Divine Unity throughout the world.[2] According to the teachings of the Qur'ān every prophet was primarily sent for this purpose,[3]

---

1 The Qur'ān VI. 163. 2 *Ibid.* XVIII. 110.
3 *Ibid.* XXI. 25.

but as corruption had crept in all these God-sent religions either through the selfishness and greed of the learned followers of such religions or through the blindness, dogmatism and ignorance of their illiterate upholders, the holy prophet of Islām claimed to have been sent to re-establish the kingdom of Heaven on earth. He was as much opposed to the plain polytheism of unbelievers and idol-worshippers as he was opposed to the three-fold godhead of God, Christ, and Gabriel, of the Christians,[1] or to the still cruder form of Trinity as conceived by the more ignorant, that of father, mother and son.[2] He has been accused of borrowing a good deal in his ideas from the so called civilised Jews, but he was no less annoyed with them for their asserting the godhead of Ezra,[3] a position to which this pious prophet was raised by his blind followers amongst the Jews, in spite of his life-long war against polytheism, which he carried on throughout his life.[4]

It is this central idea of the absolute and abstract Unity of God that forms a sort of nucleus to the doctrines of Islāmic Sufism. The Arabic word Islām itself means complete submission to the Will of Allāh. The Qur'ān tells us that this name, as referring to a particular class of people, was first used by Abraham,[5] who himself was

1 The Qur'ān IV. 17 and V. 73.
2 *Ibid.* V. 116.
3 *Ibid.* IX. 30.
4 Old Testament ' Ezra ', VII,10.
5 The Qur'ān II. 128.

a Muslim in the true sense of the word. On this account, this word appears to have some reference to the story of the sacrifice of Ishmael by his father Abraham who was so ordered by Allāh in order to test the depth of his faith. Those who know this story are well aware how pathetic it is, and what an extreme devotion to one's ideal, faith and Beloved One does it illustrate. An old man about to complete the century of his life takes out his son of thirteen, the only fruit of his long years of patience and prayers, in order to sacrifice him with his own hand! Such an act of extreme piety could not pass off uncommemorated, for the Qur'ān says, "Certainly Allāh is all knowing and thankful."[1] Allāh does not waste the acts of piety and devotion ever done by His lovers. It is this anecdote which is commemorated by the Muslims, all over the world on the day of 'Īdu'l-Aḍḥā. The faithful followers of Islām are called Muslims, because like Abraham they are required by Allāh to obey His commands unquestioningly, even though they may have to do so at the cost of their most loved and cherished possessions.

It is clear from this that Islām emphasises the importance of acts of devotion and piety. But it is as well evident from the Qur'ān and traditions that Islam did not neglect the doctrinal aspect of religion. It emphasised not only acting rightly, but

1 The Qur'ān II.158.

also holding a true belief in the different realities of the universe, and in the personalities worshipped by other religions. From this point of view it was more a creed of doctrines than a mere code of action. So far as it attached the greatest importance to right belief in and about the one and the only Creator of all things, beings, and existences, it was much more dogmatic and theoretical than any one of the previous positive religions of the world in general and of the Semites in particular. But it did not content itself only with the establishment of the dogma with which it had so vehemently started. Nor did it end like Vedantism in evolving systems of philosophy. Its aim was to beget right acting out of right thinking. After once establishing firmly the fundamental theory of the Unity of God, it enjoined its followers to act out that principle. The whole history of the origin of Islām is a progress from dogmas to individual moral action, from individual moral action to united social activity, and from united social activity to conquest and expansion. So long as the founder of Islām was in Mecca he emphasised the dogmatic aspect of the faith, but after arriving at Medina he began to preach the social aspects and the moral implications of his dogmatic faith, and it was only after his death that the policy of expansion and conquest was carried out by his followers.

There is no doubt, therefore, that Islām on the whole laid greater emphasis on acting according to the law of God, than merely philosophising. This fact is as well clear from the name that has been given to the whole system. It has been called "Sharī'ah", which is equivalent to "Divine Law", thus emphasising the systematic legal aspect of the faith. Law is very closely associated with order and organisation in a developed society. The term always implies some kind of demand on practical obedience from the members of the society for which it is brought into existence.

Sharī'ah, however, did not concern itself only with right acting, for its whole structure was supported by certain articles of faith. In a large number of verses in the Qur'ān there is a clear reference to right thinking, *i.e.*, thinking according to the Will of God. Islām therefore did not exclusively emphasise right acting or right thinking but attached due importance to each one of them according to the requirements of the occasion and according to the stage of the mental development of the individual person who sought its light and guidance.

But these references to abstract thinking were brief, and were not probably intended to occupy much time and attention of the faithful. The practical genius of the Arab race kept them in the back ground for a considerable length of time, and the early wars of the faithful left them little leisure to be tempted by mental luxuries and logical hair-splittings.

A little freedom from these civil and foreign wars and a little peace under the protection of some powerful Amir was enough to divert the mental energy of the Muslims towards evolving elaborate systems out of the brief references to certain abstract problems, most of which were barely mentioned in the Qur'ān. The result was the vast expansion of Qur'ānic and traditional literature in various directions. A huge structure of theoretical knowledge was built on the foundation of meagre references in the Qur'ān and Traditions. Development of different aspects of this literature took place under the influence of different foreign elements which were brought to bear upon the Qur'ān and Traditions, the only two original sources of Islāmic knowledge. Muslim Jurisprudence developed under the influence of Roman Law, philosophy under the influence of Aristotle, and Mysticism under the influence of Plato and Plotinus. Each thrived and expanded on a soil congenial to its progress and development. But it is an established fact that Islām had in it all the germs of the various Sufi doctrines. The Islāmic idea of the Unity of God was unanimously accepted by the Sufis as the starting point and the cardinal principle of their creed. Moreover, Islām had held out a path of direct communion with God to every individual human being. God says in the Qur'ān: "We are nearer to him (*i.e.*, to every individual human being) than even his life-vein."[1] Islām had plainly indicated that no intermediary was required to intervene between man and God. The

1 The Qur'ān L. 16.

Qur'ān says "And your Lord said, 'Call upon Me and I will answer you'."[1] Islām had, so to speak, removed the veils that were hung between the Creator and the created by the ignorant and the self-interested. Islām had unveiled the vision of the Creator for every one who had a mind to see Him. There had been many prophets and saints before the founder of Islam, and every one of them had said something or other about the Creator of the universe, but he, as the saying goes, clearly revealed the vision of God to the naked eye of the faithful. The prophet had brought about such a mental outlook among his followers that once 'Alī, his cousin and son-in-law, is reported to have said, "Even if I were to see God with my physical eyes my faith would not increase by a grain thereby."[2] The idea can thus be expressed that Allāh was a hidden treasure; He sent His beloved messenger, who took the veil away from off the human eyes and so all could see Him, and feel His presence.[3] On this foundation it was not difficult to construct an edifice. The central idea of the unity of God, combined with the possibility of every individual human being's easy and direct access to his Creator without any intermediary was stretched to its logical limits and a set of doctrines was evolved out of these principles under

---

1 The Qur'ān XL. 60. 2 "لو كشف الغطاء لما زدت يقيناً"

3 *Vide* 'Aṭṭār's Mathnawī Jawharu'dh-Dhāt, Part II, p. 410 :

"درون را با برون یکسان بکرده . بر افکنده حجابت هفت پرده"

various foreign influences. These doctrines now form the bulk of Sufi theories and Sufi literature. We shall further see how certain other practices and sayings of the prophet helped to develop these doctrines. As pointed out above, Islāmic Sufism, like many other Islāmic doctrines, assumed different forms in the different epochs of Muslim civilisation. These doctrines were modified and affected by the atmosphere in which they had their birth. It means that the beliefs, customs, and habits of the people, among whom these doctrines flourished modified them in such a way as to bring them in a line with the beliefs that were held by them prior to their adoption of the religion of Islām. In this way Sufism, to a certain extent, worked for the revival of the pre-Islāmic element among those people who had accepted Islām. The proselytism of these people to Islām was sudden, and was chiefly due to the irresistible political, military, and moral superiority of the then conquering Arabs, but the reaction was comparatively slow and was carefully concealed under the cover of religion and piety. The illiterate masses, who had hardly ever grasped the truth and essence of Islām soon came under the influence of these theories. The explanation of the curious phenomenon as to how a movement, which was originally an intellectual and philosophical one, came to be so popular among the masses, is not far to seek. The early propagandists of this movement being well aware of the strong orthodoxy of the religious views of the Muslim public of their days gave a religious colour to their reactionary tenets. The chief object of this movement, of which the popularisation of the Sufi theories formed one very important part, was political and social and aimed at doing away with the Arab supremacy in the political domain and subverting the social organisation which was built on Arab supremacy and Islāmic superiority. They appealed to the popular sentiments and based their propaganda on the principles of pre-Islāmic beliefs which were not yet entirely forgotten by the recent converts. The position at that time was something like this. The masses had embraced Islām only recently and were not prepared to hear anything against their newly adopted creed, but the old traditions which they had seen only their fathers following blindly were still alive in their memory, and were playing an important part sub-consciously in moulding their views about Islāmic doctrines.[1] The reactionaries, the original propagandists of the Sufi doctrines, interpreted the doctrines of Islām in the light of the original beliefs of the masses and thus succeeded in converting the mass opinion in their favour. It was in this way that Sufism became a popular theory, and even those who had not the mental capacity, to follow the philosophic

---

1 Dr. E. Lehmann: Mysticism in Heathendom and Christendom, p. 59.

arguments involved in the doctrines were swept away by the movement. It has been held by some western historians that originally the Sufi movement, as started by 'Abdu'llāh b. Maymūn al-Qaddāḥ, was intended to serve only a political cause. This may be true to some extent, but as a sweeping statement it cannot be justified on the grounds of historical evidence. These western scholars have, in fact, confused two movements in the Islāmic world, one started by 'Abdu'llāh b. Maymūn al-Qaddāḥ, and the other which, as they say, began with Salmān-i-Pārsī and 'Uways-i-Qarnī. The confusion appears to have arisen on account of the supposed allegiance of both the movements to the name of 'Alī, the cousin and son-in-law of the prophet.[1] But there was a vast difference in the aims and objects of the two, though the methods pursued by their supporters were almost the same. The object of the movement started by 'Abdu'llāh was political, for he wanted to destroy the Arab supremacy,[2] while the traditional movement associated with the name of Salmān and 'Uways was essentially based upon Love and devotion to God. 'Abdu'llāh had given a religious colour to his propaganda, while Salmān and 'Uways adhered to simple Islām and Islāmic practices. They and their followers had no particular worldly aims of their own to pursue, while

1 Macdonald : Muslim Theology, p. 182.

2 *Ibid.* p. 40.

'Abdu'llāh had a definite aim of overthrowing the ruling race and establishing the rule of another nation. His doctrines, therefore, were fashioned in the light of the persons whom he definitely aimed to raise high in power, while the school of 'Uways and Salmān, which can truly be called the school of Muslim saints, only aimed at teaching the esoteric meaning of the Qur'ān and the sayings of the prophet and at giving a deeper sense to the ordinary practices enjoined by Islām for the faithful.[1]

There is no doubt that the western scholars have been betrayed into this confusion by the fact that for a very long time in the Muslim history both these doctrines were upheld by the same persons. At least so was the case after philosophy began to influence the Muslim intelligentia. In their origin, no doubt, both these movements were distinct and different, but after some time they appear to have developed on much the same lines and in the same direction.[2] This development of these two movements on the same lines did not continue for a very long time. 'Abdu'llāh's movement began to die out after a few centuries, when the political objects aimed at by its author were achieved to a certain extent, and when the zeal of its active workers was exhausted; while the other movement, alleged to have been started by 'Uways, continued

1 Nicholson: A Literary History of Arabs, p. 392.

2 Ibn Khaldūn: Muqaddimah, p. 473 (Beyrout ed. 1900 A.D.)

to progress, and win converts from the orthodox section. Its principles were slowly absorbed by the strict orthodox Muslim theology and the knowledge of these doctrines was considered an additional accomplishment to the learning of the Qur'ān, Sunnah and Theology.

Sufism in Islām has suffered a good deal by its unfortunate historic association with the movement of 'Abdu'llāh, but we cannot help emphasising that this association is at the most a confusion. In order to understand Sufism clearly, and in its true light, it is essential, therefore, that it must be distinguished from the so called mystic movement of 'Abdu'llāh, which was later on revived and developed by Ḥasan b. Sabbāḥ and his assassins.[1] This movement, as has been pointed out above, was only political and therefore in our treatment of Islāmic Sufism we shall but slightly refer to it, because many doctrines of Sufism itself have undergone a considerable change under the influence of the intense propaganda of the so called mystics of 'Abdu'llāh's school. We shall only study the principles, the origin, the development and the present offshoots of Sufism, which are based upon Islām and Islāmic doctrines, that is, those which have appeared after the advent of Islām. As the subject is very vast and it is impossible to treat it in all its possible developments and details, we will limit our discussion only to

1 Macdonald: Muslim Theology, p. 49.

its development among those people that profess Islām as their religion. For the sake of convenience, we will divide the development of these doctrines among the Muslims into different stages in their historical order and try to find out what particular form was taken by these doctrines at each stage, what external influences were at work at that time, and how far they had gone astray from their original source at that particular stage. In other words, we will try to explore how much of each of these doctrines at a particular stage was Islāmic and how much was due to the non-Islāmic and foreign influences.

CHAPTER II

THE EARLY BEGINNINGS OF SUFISM IN ISLAM AS ILLUSTRATED IN THE PRACTICES OF THE PROPHET.

Each Sufi order claims that the doctrines and practices prevalent among the adherents of that order originated in the days of the founder of Islām. There is no doubt that the mode of his living warrants that claim to a certain extent. He led an extremely simple life, consciously avoiding all luxuries and showing complete indifference to the ordinary pleasures of an average man. He preached the message of Allāh during the day and prayed to Him for a major portion of the night[1] Heaps of wealth, and a number of valuable presents were sent to him by the rulers of different countries but he did not retire to sleep until he had disposed of in charity the last farthing of the uncountable riches. He purchased his own things in the market. He stitched his own clothes, mended his own shoes, swept his own house when so many of his followers were ever ready to lay down their lives at his simple nod.[2] In the battlefield he dug ditches with his own hands like an ordinary soldier, although every body on the field considered him as his spiritual leader and guide. Whenever

1 The Qur'ān LXXIII.20.

2 Ghazāli: Kimyā-i-Sa'ādat, Navalkishore Press, 1882, p. 280.

he judged he decided with justice, and whenever his advice was sought he advised to the best interest of the seeker. He spoke nothing but the truth. He did not abuse nor did he curse.[1] He never took revenge for any injury done to his person. When once asked to curse the people that had almost wounded him to death he replied, "I have been sent by Allāh not to curse but to be a blessing here and hereafter."[2] He entered Mecca as a conqueror and the Meccans were waiting every moment for an order of general massacre, but the first thing that he did was to proclaim a general amnesty to all. It is said about him that during the whole period of his prophethood which extended over twenty-three years he did not take full meals even once.[3] When wealth was pouring in from every direction, in his own cottage he did not possess more than a mattress to sleep on and an earthen pitcher full of water to make ablution with and to drink.[4] He fasted continuously for months together, and slept little at night, but none of these self-imposed hardships ever hindered him from travelling long distances in the scorching sun of Arabia, nor from preaching long sermons whenever he found an occasion to do so. In short, he was a man who did most and claimed least. He is made to say in the Qur'ān like other prophets,

1 Bukhārī Ṣaḥīḥ : Kitābu'l-Ādāb.

2 'Iyāḍ: Shifā, p. 47.

3 Bukhārī Ṣaḥīḥ : Kitābu'l Aṭ'imah.

4 Ibn Sa'd: Ṭabaqāt, Vol. VIII, p. 136, Ed. Sachau.

"Whatever reward I have asked of you, that is only for yourself (*i.e.*, I do not ask you any reward for my services), my reward is only with Allāh."[1]

All these things look strange and superhuman to us who have been living in luxury and ease, but they well illustrate the extent to which human nature can progress by slow and steady spiritual activity. Not only in practice but also in theory he gave a deep spiritual significance to all terms of ordinary meaning. Thus he is reported to have defined goodness or "Iḥsān" as a mode of worshipping Allāh, a way of complete absorption in praying to Him. "Thou shouldst pray to God' he said 'as if thou sawest Him and if thou canst not see Him, He seeth thee."[2] It is on this definition of Iḥsān that many Sufis have built their theory of devotion. This definition indicates the prophet's theory of spiritual good and was rightly made a starting point for spiritual theories by Sufis. When one is thus face to face with his Almighty Creator, one's mind is likely to oscillate between two points. An awe of the vast infinite power of the Almighty mixed up with the consciousness of one's own weaknesses, from which none can claim to be free, possesses the mind along with the feelings of all forgiving pity, kindness and extreme love of the Creator for His creatures. In short, in His presence the mind wavers between

1 The Qur'ān XXXIV. 47.

2 Bukhārī: Ṣaḥīḥ, Kitāb'ul-Imān.

two passions of hope and fear. Thus the mental attitude of the faithful should be neither that of total despondence nor that of complete security. The Qur'ān also speaks in the similar language and lays down that the path of virtue lies between fear and hope. It says, "Despair not of Allāh's mercy, surely none despairs of Allāh's mercy but the unbelieving people."[1] Again it says, "O you who believe, be careful (or afraid) of Allāh with the care which is due to Him,"[3] *i.e.*, to the extreme extent. Again in another place while praising the deeds of Zacharias and his son John, the Qur'ān says, "Surely they used to hasten in deeds of goodness and call upon us, hoping and fearing; and they were humble before us."[3] The Qur'ān is still more clear on this point when it says, "and call on Him fearing and hoping."[4]

It is this definition of prayer that has helped the doctrine of Ecstacy and Rapture to become so popular among the Muslim Sufis. According to this definition the lowest grade of devotion and prayer is the consciousness of the fact that one's Lord is watching his movements and knowing the inmost secrets of his heart. Any person conscious of this watchfulness of his Creator is sure to desist from evil actions, nay even from evil thoughts. This consciousness once awakened forms a very

1 The Qur'ān XII. 87. 2 *Ibid.* III. 101.
3 *Ibid.* XXI. 90. 4 *Ibid.* VII. 55.

strong foundation for a healthy moral character. It becomes a check on our evil propensities much more strong than any fear of the public exposure of our evil acts can be. It is possible to commit an evil act and to conceal it from a human eye but it is impossible to conceal it from the all-seeing, all-watching, and all-judging eye, provided you only become conscious of this fact. Once you believe in this all-watching eye, there is a natural inclination to shun the evil, and this very belief begins to work as a strong check on your character. It is in this sense that prayer can reform the character of a person. The Qur'ān says, "Surely prayer keeps (one) away from indecency and evil."[1] But it is to be remembered that prayers can yield this result only if one prays with the consciousness that his all-seeing Creator is watching his movements. When the mere consciousness of His presence can affect human mind so powerfully, what would be the condition of that man, who loves Him with his whole heart, at the time when he goes into His presence and meets Him face to face? He would be all rapture, absorption, emotion and joy. Thus all the fanciful movements, strange dances and other instances of vulgar ecstacy that we find among the illiterate mass of dervishes, can be explained to have developed from this belief. Such practices are nothing but vulgar and unintelligent physical

1 The Qur'ān XXIX. 45.

expressions of the internal emotions and joys which they say they feel at the time of meeting their Beloved One. It is true that certain saints have been observed to fall senseless when possessed by the emotion of extreme love, and some are even reported to have died under the spell of ecstacy.

Sufis freely quote anecdotes from the life of the prophet and his companions, particularly 'Alī, the cousin and son-in-law of the prophet, to support the view that the doctrine of ecstacy or rapture originated in the days of the prophet and his companions. It is reported in the traditions that once the prophet was offering his prayers in the Ka'bah when an unbeliever named 'Uqbah b. Abī Mu'ayṭ brought the entrails of a big camel and placed them on his back and shoulders while he was down in prostration before his Allāh. It is said that he was so busy and so much absorbed in his prayers that he did not feel it in the least and was quite unaware of the occurrence until his daughter who happened to pass that way removed the burden from his back.[1] It is this complete absorption in prayers, say the Sufis, which is the foundation of ecstacy and rapture. Again, it is reported about 'Alī that once an arrow struck deep into his body. People tried to get it out but could not succeed, as it was too deep to be extracted without extreme pain. He then began to say his

1 Aḥmad b. Ḥanbal. Musnad, Vol. I, p. 393, Cairo 1330. also Bukhārī: Ṣaḥīḥ: Kitābu'l-Wuḍū'.

prayers during which it was extracted after a deep operation with a sword. It is said that on account of his complete absorption he did not feel any pain until he had finished his prayers and seen the blood gushing out of the wound.

Sufis of the later age did not consider this absorption necessary only at the time of canonical prayers but also at the occasion of Dhikr and meditation which were given an importance equal to the obligatory prayers by many of them. Dhikr literally means remembering Allāh. In popular language, it means repeating the name of Allāh. The Qur'ān says, "Remember Allāh much, that you may be successful."[1] Again, it says, "O You who believe! Remember Allāh, remembering frequently."[2] The Qur'ān mentions ninety-nine different names of God and according to another version as many as nine hundred and ninety-nine. Each name indicates a particular attribute of Allāh and fits in with the context in which it is mentioned in the Qur'ān. This topic will be taken up later on; for the time being let it suffice here to point out that the early followers of the prophet interpreted this verse about Dhikr in a very broad sense.[3] A judge deciding the disputes among Muslims according to the code of Sharī'ah was performing his duty to Allāh and was thus remembering his Crea-

1 The Qur'ān LXII. 10. 2 *Ibid.* XXXIII. 41.

3 Mujaddid Aḥmad Sirhindī : Letters, Vol. I. Letter 25.

tor. It was a form of worship for him and in addition to his reward for ordinary obligatory prayers he would also get a reward for discharging his duties to his fellow human beings if he did them according to the orders of Allāh. Similarly a soldier fighting in the name of Allāh, for defending his faith, country or the faithful, was performing Dhikr. It is evident from this that though his ordinary prayers during his active service are reduced to half the usual, this reduction does not stand in the way of his attaining a high place in the favour of Allāh. The Qur'ān is full with the praise and promises of reward for those who fight in the way of Allāh. It says, "Surely Allāh loves those who fight in His way in ranks."[1] Similarly a Caliph leading his armies to defend the land, property and lives of the faithful is also performing his Dhikr. The idea was that anything done in the name of Allāh, conforming to His law and orders, was tantamount to remembering Allāh or performing Dhikr. It was considered something equivalent to the ethical conception of performing one's duty or discharging one's function of life, strictly according to the message and commands of the almighty Allāh.

Later Sufis began to attach greater importance to the popular meaning of the term Dhikr, thus vastly limiting the scope of the above quoted verse of the Qur'ān. It was on account of this limited

1 The Qur'ān LXI. 4.

interpretation that the later Sufis invented so many novel ways of calling out the name of Allāh.[1] Howling, singing and dancing dervishes are distinguished according to the different modes of performing their Dhikr.

The early followers of the prophet regarded all forms of prayers other than compulsory prayers as "Nawāfil", *i.e.*, works of supererogation. The term literally means plundering, but technically it has come to mean "Plundering the bounty and kindness of God". Islām used this term in the sense of doing good in addition to the performance of one's obligatory duties or "Farā'iḍ". Islām enjoins a universal minimum of positive duties to be discharged by every individual who enters into its fold and gives them the name of "Farā'iḍ". As for example, the law obliges every one of the faithful to part with one-fortieth of his savings at the end of every year in favour of the poor members of the community. If one does it, he is simply discharging his obligations, but if he gives one-twentieth of his savings in alms then he doubly earns the favour of his all-merciful God, by this additional voluntary charity, which would be technically known as a nafl.

The prophet had drawn the attention of his followers to the supererogatory deeds by himself sticking strictly to the midnight prayers.[2] It

1 Brown: Dervishes, Chap. 3.

2 Bukhārī: Ṣaḥīḥ, Bābu't-Tahajjud bi'l-Layl.

is to be noted, however, that the early followers of the prophet interpreted the word nafl in a very general sense and understood from it any good action performed over and above one's duties. The later Sufis restricted the word to its narrow sense of saying prayers in addition to the fixed prayers, just as they had limited the meaning of the word Dhikr to only repeating the names of Allāh.

All these illustrations show that in later days many of the Islāmic institutions lost their original meaning though they still retained the same old garb of name or outward appearance. This change took place very slowly and imperceptibly, and was responsible, in no small degree, for undermining the strength and vitality of the Muslim community.

If this process had been limited merely to theoretical basis of Islām like beliefs and prayers, probably it would not have proved very harmful. But the new acquaintance with the Dialectics of the Greeks, and constant civil wars resulting in a desire for relaxation, did not allow the peacefully inclined persons for long to desist from applying their newly acquired logical acumen to the material and fundamental principles and practices of the faith to which they claimed to belong. The climax was reached, when the terms like "Unity of God" and "Religious War" were made to bear connotations which their author would have utterly repudiated in his time.

The term "Religious War" or "Defence War" has been used in the Qur'ān on different occasions in different contexts.[1] The Qur'ān says, "Make war in the name of Allāh with your person and property."[2] Again, it says "Permission (to fight) is given to those upon whom war is made because they are oppressed."[3] Again on another occasion the Qur'ān mentions it as an obligatory duty when it says, "Fighting is enjoined on you."[4] To the early Muslims these verses conveyed that whenever the unbelievers attacked the Muslims and oppressed them it was incumbent upon them to repel the attack and defend themselves. Muslims are in duty bound to defend their freedom of religion, conscience, family and state. Nay even if they find any person or any nation unreasonably oppressed by another person or nation they are morally bound to help and support the weak party.[5] For this purpose they are enjoined to spend their wealth, to collect subscriptions for which an example was set by the prophet himself, and to go to the battlefield personally.

The term Jihād, as its root jahd implies, means to make an effort. The Qur'ān used it in the same wide sense of making efforts in the path of Allāh.[6] The Sufis limited it to only one kind

1 The Qur'ān III. 166. 2 *Ibid.* LXI. 11.
3 *Ibid.* XXII. 39. 4 *Ibid.* II. 216.
5 M. Muhammad Ali: Translation of the Qur'ān, note 276.
6 *Ibid.* note 1073.

of effort, that of fighting against one's own evil self, against the Satanic element in human nature. For early believers the term included every hardship that one had to bear in the path of Allāh, and every sacrifice one had to make for His sake. Even Tablīgh or preaching of Islām was considered to be a kind of Jihād, since it involved some kind of activity for the sake of Allāh. Later Sufis did not interpret the term in this wide sense but were inclined to exclude every concrete action out of its meaning. Consequently we find that the preaching of Islām was totally neglected by the Sufis of the later age as a class.

An extraordinary ingenuity was displayed by the Sufis in this connection by classifying Jihād into two kinds—" Jihād-i-Akbar " and " Jihād-i-Asghar ".[1] Jihād-i-Asghar (holy war of less importance) was defined as the ordinary war referred to in the Qur'ān and Sunnah, that is, a war fought for defending one's home, land, religion and honour whenever attacked by the aggressors. Jihād-i-Akbar (holy war of greater importance) was defined as a struggle against one's own Demon-spirit, and keeping watch over one's own heart against the attack of Satan who misguided the human beings through evil suggestions. Self-control was exalted over the discipline of the battlefield. A person who was not suffi-

---

1 Rūmī : Book 1 "قد رجعنا من جهاد الاصغریم بانبی اندر جهادِ اکبریم" or Muḥyu'd-Dīn b. al-'Arabī : al-Futūḥāt'ul-Makkiyyah : Vol. II. Chap. on Mujāhadah, Vol. II.

ciently disciplined in self-command had no right to go to fight against unbelievers. In this way, the self slowly began to mean simply an inner principle. The mind turned its gaze inwards and as a result the relationship of the self with the external world was weakened.

The torch of light instead of being shown to others, who might have been benefitted more by it than the torch-bearer himself, was turned inwards to guide one's own heart. Thus the first advice that a Shaikh gave to his disciple was "First reform thyself and then try to reform others." The Sufis claim to derive this principle from the verse of the Qur'ān that lays down, "It is most hateful to Allāh that you should say that which you do not do."[1]

There is no doubt that this principle is a sure safeguard against presumptuousness. It is a definite principle on the basis of which the claims of saintship can be judged with some certainty. A large number of stories are given in books on Sufism to support this theory, that it is impossible to reform others unless one first reforms one's self. An interesting story which historically is of very doubtful authenticity is related about 'Alī in this connection.[2] It is said that once a woman went to

---

1 The Qur'ān LXI. 3.

2 It is associated with the names of different saints in the history of Taṣawwuf, sometimes with the name of Niẓāmu'ddīn of Delhi,

him with her son and requested the saint to advise her young son not to take excessive sugar against which the physician had warned him. It is reported, that the saint asked her to bring her son after a few days. When she went with her son next time he spoke to the young boy exhorting him to give up the habit,* and it is said that after that time he never took sugar in harmful quantities again. When the saint was asked why he had postponed the affair, he replied that before that he himself was in the habit of taking excessive sugar, so at that time his words could have produced no effect. Therefore first of all he gave up the habit himself and then made an effort to reform that young boy. From this it can be inferred that the preachings of a man who does not act according to his own principles cannot reform any one else.

In theory this principle appears to be quite sound, but its results proved to be fatal and disastrous. The propagation of Islām was seriously hampered by it. It practically stopped Jihād, and indirectly hindered the progress of Muslim jurisprudence. Its influence was far-reaching, and the character of this influence was to check and counteract the growing tendencies of Muslims towards progress in the various

sometimes with the name of Khwājah Naqshband, and sometimes with that of ʻAlī. I have not been able to find it in any standard work, but every Sufi knows it. I have quoted it only by way of explaining the practical view of later Sufis.

domains of life and activity. It was also responsible, much more than all the Qur'ānic descriptions of the terrors of Hell, in bringing about quietism which the Western writers on Mysticism consider to be the source of mystic tendencies among the Muslims.[1]

Even on psychological grounds this principle is not very sound. There is no possibility of setting a limit to the progress of an individual human soul. If a man decides first to develop his own soul and then to preach the Gospel of Truth to others, the time of conveying the mission to others will never come. It is a strange paradox of human nature that the more a man progresses morally the more he feels himself wanting in goodness, and the more he becomes conscious of his shortcomings. Just as a rich man desires more in proportion to his possessions, similarly with the moral progress of a man his standard of judging his own conduct rises higher. His conscience becomes more delicate. He begins to feel even his trifling shortcomings, which an ordinary unreflective human being would pass over very lightly. It is a well known paradox of Ethics, that the nearer one approaches his ideal the further away it flies from him.

This paradox explains the various verses of the Qur'ān wherein prophets are represented as praying

1 Macdonald: Muslim Theology, p. 177; Nicholson: Mysticism in Islām, Chaps. I and II; and Dr. Lehmann: Mysticism in Heathendom and Christendom, p. 61.

to God for forgiveness. The prophets being as a class superior to others spiritually and morally, are always conscious of their trifling shortcomings much more than others. Consequently they pray for forgiveness even more than their followers.

However, it was intended to be only an illustration of the fact how Sufis, particularly in later days, went farther away from the real teachings of the prophet. The next step they took was to give up the practice of giving alms, which was enjoined upon every Muslim. The Sufis were becoming ascetics. Their activities were slowly becoming limited to Takyah and Ḥujrah,[1] and they were slowly cutting themselves aloof from the world and the worldly people. Consequently every day they were becoming less self-dependent and more dependent upon their disciples for their livelihood. Those of their disciples who were carrying on trade or other professions and were well-to-do, were taught to part with a portion of their earnings in favour of their Spiritual Guides. In return they were to receive the favour of God and the blessings of their saint. Masses who were daily becoming ignorant of the real teachings of Islām, accepted it as a very convenient mode of gaining the favour of Allāh. Thus the asceticism

---

1 Takyah is a portion of a mausoleum, set apart for the residence of the successor of a saint, and Ḥujrah is a portion of a mosque set apart for the residence of the Imām or a person who leads prayers in the mosque.

of Sufis damaged the Islāmic principle of Zakāt in two ways: firstly, by driving a section of intelligent and intellectual Muslims out of the economical struggle and thus decreasing the general earning capacity of the total class, and secondly, by diverting a quantity of alms towards the support of undeserving persons who could earn their own livelihood by means of other productive ways. This deprived a large number of deserving and poor members of the community of the help which was their legitimate due.

Moreover, the dependence of the spiritual class on the earning members of the society was demoralising in many other ways. Firstly, it created a special class of priesthood; secondly, it made spiritual favours saleable commodities, and thirdly, it made spiritual leadership a profession, which as such drew people of inferior intelligence to its fold, and lowered the status and prestige of sainthood.

In this way we find the practice of giving alms or Zakāt almost neglected by the later Sufis. They were themselves unable to give any, as they had taken to asceticism and were no more earning members of the community. Thus they really divested the institution of its true value and usefulness.

Islām, as a religion, had forbidden ascetic practices. There are many verses in the Qur'ān which definitely lay down that to run away from the society or to abstain, without any reasonable excuse, from the use of things permitted by law, is an act of impiety. One full chapter[1] of the Qur'ān is devoted to demonstrate that the prophet had no right to take a vow against the use of a thing permitted by God. Authentic evidence relates this chapter to an anecdote in the life of the prophet, that he left off taking honey at the request of one of his wives.[2] The Qur'ān expresses this principle still more clearly on another occasion by laying down, "Say: Who has prohibited the embellishment of Allāh, which He has brought forth for His servants, and the good provisions."[3] This verse is very significant inasmuch as it enunciates an important principle that it is God alone, the Creator of all things and the best Spiritual Guide, Who has the right to fix for His creatures what is forbidden and what is permissible.[4] This verse is intended to close for

---

1 The Qur'ān, Chap. LXVI; and Bukhārī: Ṣaḥīḥ, Kitāb Tafsīrul'-Qur'ān.

2 There are two versions: one related by 'Ā'ishah about honey, and the other by 'Umar regarding the prophet's giving up his visit to his wives. I accept the formeras more creditable for the following reasons:

(a) That 'Ā'ishah had a greater possibility of knowing a domestic incident.

(b) It goes against her, as, according to her report, she was also involved in it, and one does not report a thing against one's self unless it is quite true.

3 The Qur'ān VII. 32. 4 *Ibid.* X. 59.

ever the practice of giving up the use of certain things in the name of religion and God, for this practice introduces an element of personal likes and dislikes for certain things. It was these individual likes or dislikes that were taken by younger generations as inseparable parts of religion, and thus undermined the fundamental principles and the pristine purity of the revealed religions. This principle was intended to have a very far-reaching safeguard against corruption in Islām. On *a priori* grounds as well, God alone knows what things should be used and why. The Qur'ān says, "Eat and drink and be not extravagant."[1] On another occasion it says, "O men! eat the lawful and good things out of what is in the earth and do not follow the footsteps of the Devil......"[2] Similarly it says, "O you who believe, eat of the good things that We have provided you with and give thanks to Allāh".[3] The Qur'ān is still more clear when it lays down, "O you who believe! do not forbid to (yourself) the good (pure) things which Allāh has made lawful for you and do not exceed the limits".[4] The prophet was quite emphatic on this point as it appears from his well known saying, "There is no asceticism in Islām."[5]

The reason for this principle appears to be something like this, that a Muslim as the very word

---

1 The Qur'ān VII. 31. 2 *Ibid.* II. 168.

3 *Ibid.* II. 172. 4 *Ibid.* V. 87, 88.

5 Aḥmad b. Ḥanbal: Musnad, Vol. VI, p. 226 (Cairo 1330).

implies has no will of his own. He eats and drinks not what he likes but what his Beloved Creator likes for him and His likings can be known by what He has permitted or forbidden to eat and drink in the Qur'ān through His Messenger. In this way if one surrenders his will unto His orders and likings he attains such a nearness to Him that He alone becomes the mind, the will and the motive of all his actions, as Rūmī has well said in his famous verse, "That voice is absolutely of the king himself although it may proceed from the throat of 'Abdu'llāh."[1]

At this stage of love, the creature has no choice of his own. He dare not use anything forbidden by Law, nor forbid anything for himself which has been allowed by Law. The Law or the Command of his Beloved One becomes the supreme principle of his life and he is guided by this alone, rather than by the frail and fickle instincts and passions of human nature. The Supreme Reason of the All Just guides him in everything. He judges and chooses according to the Supreme Will of Allāh and not according to the blind impulse of his own nature.

This was the turning point in the history of Sufism in Islām. This very devotion to the Supreme Will became the basis of the extreme

---

1 « مطلق آن آواز خود از شه بود گرچه از حلقوم عبد الله بود »
It is an effort to explain revelation, but Muslims as a rule do not accept this theory.

asceticism of the Sufis. A Sufi would claim to act according to the Will of Allāh in a way much more austere than an ordinary pious Muslim. A Sufi would say that he had absolutely no will of his own, not even to choose out of the permitted things. Even among the permitted things he chooses what his Allāh wants. It is the Will of God that prescribes things for him in every detail of life. He would deprive himself of any power of choice, even among things lawful and permitted.

This view of the Sufis differs from that of the early followers of the prophet in a very important respect. When a companion of the prophet would say that he was acting according to the Will of Allāh he would mean by it that his action conformed to the law as given in the Qur'ān or as explained by the words or the actions of the prophet. While a Sufi when using the same words would mean by them that he was acting as Allāh directly guided him to act. A Sufi would claim a direct communion with God without the intervention of the Law. So according to the ordinary view of the Muslims the only way of ascertaining the liking of Allāh is possible through His revelation, while a Sufi would claim to know His will directly through ecstacy.

The difference in these two ways of seeking guidance through His will is quite clear and important. In the former case the idea of Law is more prominent, while in the latter it is self which becomes more important. In the former case, the action depends upon the interpretation of the law, while in the latter the individual whim, personal caprice, lower animal instincts and passions may unconsciously lead a person to moral and spiritual destruction. It is not very unlikely that the claim of Manṣūr b. Ḥallāj that he was identical to the Supreme Truth was an illustration of this kind of misguided view of direct communion. It can be laid down as a general rule that to seek the Will of Allāh except through the help of the Qur'ān and the traditions of the prophet is beset with snares and pitfalls, in any one of which the seeker may fall without his being consciously aware of his having been lost. This kind of independence from law is likely to degrade into obedience to the lower self and the worship of one's own desires.[1]

But it does not mean that there is no possibility of direct communion with God. Islām was the first religion in the world to open a way for direct communion. In India and Persia, in Greece and Rome, among the Jews and the Christians, there had sprung up a class of saints and priests who had monopolised communion with God, gods, deities or other superhuman powers. This special class always tried to monopolise the spiritual blessings to themselves and to their offspring, with the result that the majority of the society had either to go without any, or had to beg them as a favour from

1 The Qur'ān XLV. 23.

the members of this privileged class. This class in order to preserve themselves as a class always preached to the people that it was impossible to have direct communion with God except through the intervention of one of the members of the class either living or dead. It was on account of this intervention that the more influential priests were raised to divinity by those of their blind followers who had first approached them only to be guided to the Almighty God. In this way the theory of the intervention of saints[1] was responsible for introducing polytheism even among the monotheistic societies.[2]

Islām abolished this principle completely and denounced the possibility of anybody's intervening on behalf of any other person before Allāh, on the day of judgment. The Qur'ān says, "Who is he that can intercede with Him but by His permission."[3] Again the Qur'ān emphasises it by saying, "O believers spend out of what We have given you before the day comes in which there is no bargaining, nor any friendship nor intercession."[4] There is a large number of verses in the Qur'ān that clearly lay down that everybody is responsible

1 The theory of Redemption is not exactly the same as that of Intervention which is discussed here, and of which Redemption is only one form. Redemption necessarily implies an idea of sin which is to be redeemed, while Intervention indicates the dispensation of heavenly favours through saints, in addition to mere redemption.

2 The Qur'ān IX. 31. 3 *Ibid.* II. 255.

4 *Ibid.* II. 254.

for his own deeds. It says,[1] "No bearer of burden shall bear the burden of another, and that man shall have nothing but what he strives for."[2] It lays down still more clearly, "Or, have they taken intercessors besides Allāh? Say: what! even though they did not ever have control over anything, nor did they understand. Say: Allāh's is the intercession altogether; His is the Kingdom of the Heavens and the earth."[3]

Islām's renunciation of this theory was based upon a thorough understanding of, and a keen insight into, the past history of religions and human spiritual consciousness. History had shown how innocent and truthful prophets like Christ could be deified under its influence. It was also responsible for introducing the custom of worshipping the souls of their forefathers in many ancient tribes. This theory is a blind advocate of authority, forbidding everything that goes against it. Its upholder abhors independence of thought. In this way it creates a slave mentality and undermines the progress and originality of the spiritual faculty. Under its influence genius is strangled and progress set back. It destroys the faculty of independent criticism, for it never allows it to be exercised.

Islām saw these things clearly and therefore denounced the theory of Intervention altogether. It announced in very unambiguous and unmistakable

1 The Qur'ān II. 286. 2 *Ibid.* LIII. 38, 39.

3 *Ibid.* XXXIX. 43, 44.

terms that none shall be able to save from Allāh, that none can intercede for others before Him, and that no intervention shall be accepted from any one on the day of judgment.[1] The idea of intervention of the Shaikh that we find prevalent among the Sufis of the later age has nothing in common with the original attitude of Islām towards this belief. It appears to have developed among the Sufis side by side with their rise as a separate class monopolising all the spiritual good to themselves. This separation of the Sufis from the rest of the Muslims was due to the fact that a large number of Sufis had accepted Sufism as a profession and had taken to asceticism. The history of various positive religions informs us that this belief in the intervention of certain personalities creeps in only when a religion is decaying and degenerating and when its grasp on the minds of its followers becomes slack. The reason for this phenomenon is not far to seek. It loosens the responsibility of the individuals with respect to their moral and spiritual duties. Nobody will like to bother himself about his moral and spiritual welfare and obligations, if he can just buy them by paying a few coins or by doing homage to someone else. It takes away the feelings of personal responsibility, thus suggesting easy means of keeping away the painful consciousness of one's own sins. But by weakening the

1 The Qur'ān II. 48.

feelings of moral and spiritual responsibility it also reduces the grasp of religion and morality on consciousness almost to nothing. It is not, therefore, too much to say that under the influence of this theory the Christian world has lost all religious consciousness. Probably it is due to this that those Sufi orders that have accepted it are fast losing the true consciousness of religion.

But the theory of the intervention of the law as suggested by Islām is quite different from the theory discussed above. The law is God's command. He has ordered His faithful creatures to act according to it. The Muslims consider the Law of the Qur'ān as the last, final and conclusive expression of the Word of God. The Qur'ān alone conveys the Will of Allāh to His worshippers. Direct communion with Him is highly laudable but without the help of the Qur'ān and the Traditions it is beset with the snares of Satan. Human passions, human aspirations and human weaknesses beset the seeker with the worst sins without the help of the Law, which is the only touchstone that never fails to give the correct estimation of all such communions. It serves the purpose of a right corrective at every stage of the spiritual flight.[1] This testing and checking of one's spiritual flight according to the standard of the Qur'ānic Law is called the theory of the "Intervention of the Law". There is no possibility of any undesirable results

1 Mujaddid Aḥmad Sirhindī; Letters 36 and 52.

by the acceptance of this theory as opposed to the theory of the intervention of persons which, as we have already seen, is sure to result in polytheism, mental degradation, and in complete and blind reliance on authority. The prophet is reported to have preached this theory by saying, "On the day of judgment, the Qur'ān (the Law) and fasting (good actions) will intercede before Allāh on behalf of the believer."[1]

Lately there has been a revival of this theory of the intervention of holy persons among almost all the orders of the Sufis, on account of the influence of other religions like Christianity and Brahmanism. Later on, we shall find that the effect of such influences on Islāmic mysticism has not been very wholesome on the whole.

Take the institution of begging, for instance. The prophet had done his best to abolish it by various ways, and he had succeeded to a great extent. But the later Sufis revived it under the pretence of renouncing the world. They began to live upon the alms and charity of their credulous rich followers. Sufis appear to have revived it under the influence of Buddhistic mendicants.

The early Sufis as a rule earned their own livelihood and never accepted any alms or charity from their followers or from any other persons. Even in our own days, there are many Sufis

---

1 Aḥmad b. Ḥanbal : Musnad, Vol. II. 174 (Cairo 1330).

who are strongly opposed to the acceptance of alms. But in the early days of Islām it was a general rule, while at present there are only few exceptional instances of those who labour fo rtheir living. The attitude of the prophet on this point was uncompromising. He had forbidden his Āl (a term which in the technique of the Qur'ān conveys the notion of both descendents and followers) from accepting any kind of charity for their livelihood. An anecdote is related about him which bears out his strong attitude on this point. A person brought to the prophet a basketful of dates which he said was the fortieth part of his annual harvest, and requested him to distribute them among the poor and the needy. A grandchild of the prophet who happened to be there took one date out of the heap and placed it in his mouth, as little children are wont to do. As soon as the prophet saw him doing it, he thrust his finger into his mouth and extracted the date out, saying "The alms are forbidden for me and for my Āl."[1]

His attitude towards asceticism was no less uncompromising. He was highly social and evidently it could not be otherwise, as the mission of his life was to reform the society, which he could never do if he had become a recluse. Asceticism in its extreme form of seclusion is highly prejudicial to the mission of social reformation. In seclusion even the term self-reformation is shorn

1 Bukhārī: Ṣaḥiḥ, Bābu Wujūbi'z-zakāt.

of all its true meaning, because when there are no temptations to overcome and the will is never exercised, real character never develops. As intellect develops by grappling and overcoming mental difficulties, so does character develop by overcoming temptations rather than by avoiding them. You would not call that person a good mathematician who, instead of solving the difficult problems, would simply keep them away from his attention. Similarly it is difficult to call that person a good man who, instead of performing his duties of manhood, would simply avoid them.

From this discussion it is not difficult to conclude that the practices prevalent among the present Sufis are not sanctioned by the traditions of Islām. It clearly proves that the Sufism of to-day is highly degenerate and cannot be justified and warranted from the practices of the founder of Islām. Nor is there any doubt that for practices like reclusion and begging the Muslim Sufis are not a little indebted to Rāhibs and Mendicants who had gone so far as to build monasteries for the purpose of retirement from the society.

We cannot pass over the institution of asceticism without discussing its merits. Asceticism is not totally valueless. It possesses disciplinary value which cannot be equalled by any other of the methods that have been tried so far for the reformation of character. True, it does not become a man to throw off the difficulties behind his back and run away from them instead of looking them in the face, still some measure of training and discipline is essential to start with. It is our experience of every day life that those, who throw themselves headlong into the sea of temptations without sufficient previous moral training, become moral wrecks. It is safe, therefore, that before entering into the battlefield of temptations one must undergo some kind of moral discipline. Asceticism serves this purpose. Just as a mathematician cannot solve the difficult problems of Mathematics without going through its initial stages, so it is desirable to undergo some kind of moral training before entering the struggle and temptations of life.

It must be noticed, however, that asceticism is useful only as a preparation, as a means to something higher. Any person, who makes it the end of his life, acquires a morbid and cynic disposition, which is highly prejudicial to the harmony and sweetness of life. As an end of life, therefore, asceticism is harmful and defeats its own purpose. To stick to it beyond a particular period of life is destructive for the right formation and smooth progress of character. In this respect probably the practice of old Hindū sages to divide life into four equal parts and to spend the first part as an ascetic scholar was the best way to get most out of this unhealthy institution on the whole. It is evident, therefore, that upto a certain period of life asceticism serves the purpose of a very useful moral discipline. But it cannot be recommended for any large section of humanity, because if practised on a large scale it would disintegrate and dissolve the society altogether. In its extreme form it is harmful to the social qualities of heroism and sympathy. No doubt, it develops the power of contemplation and concentration, but often at the cost of more fine and delicate human qualities, which go to make up real life.

This statement is clearly borne out by the biography of the prophet himself. Before the declaration of his ministry he often visited a cave known by the name of Ḥirā.[1] There he sat and meditated for days together. But after the fortieth year of his life when he declared himself to be a prophet he gave up seclusion, and instead of confining himself into a cave he began to visit assemblies, like fairs, festivals and the markets of busy towns. Now his character was formed and he would not yield to the temptations of the priceless offers of riches, leadership and complete sovereignty over all the tribes of Arabia, which the Quraish were unanimously making to him provided he gave up his preaching the new religion.[2] He was strong enough to refuse and say " Even if they were to place the sun on my right hand and the moon on my left so that I should

1 Bukhārī : Ṣaḥīḥ, Chap. on "The beginning of the Waḥy".

2 Ibn Hishām : Sīrah, p. 268 ; Cairo edition of 1329 A.H. (Published by Khairiyah Press).

give up this mission, I would not give it up, until God made it manifest or I perished."[1]

There is another point against the institution of asceticism. If every person, spiritually and morally great, takes to asceticism the society would become a den of demons devoid of all goodness and morality. It would become a pestilence to be avoided rather than a pleasure to be eagerly sought. The object of all the prophets and reformers has been to establish the Kingdom of Heaven on earth, *i.e.*, to make social life on earth as pure and spiritual as the society of Angels in the Heavens. Social reformation was the chief object of Muḥammad's mission, for the Qur'ān says about him, "We have not sent thee, but as a mercy to (all) the nations."[2] A universal asceticism, therefore, would simply defeat the Creator's purpose and would make the mission of the prophets altogether futile.

But instead of extreme and harmful asceticism another one of healthy kind is also possible. We have already seen that an extreme asceticism which appears in the form of seclusion in Takyah, monastery or temple is highly prejudicial to the fair development of the individual character as well as to the human society in general. We have also seen that it is not totally useless, and that upto a particular limit it would serve the purpose of a moral discipline. Now we should see whether the

1 *Ibid.* p. 215.

2 The Qur'ān XXI. 107.

principle can be adopted without its defects and whether such an asceticism which can serve the purpose of a good discipline without destroying the society has ever been conceived by any one of the religious systems. Islām and its founder had really taught this kind of beneficial ascetic discipline. It can best be expressed in the words of Rūmī, "Water in the boat causes its destruction, while the same water is the cause of its movement when underneath it."[1] In simpler words, "Live in the world, but let not the world live in thy heart." The expression sounds rather strange and paradoxical, and it must since it is uncommon, none the less it is true to the letter. It simply means that the essential characteristic of a real ascetic is not to run away from the world or to shun the society but to become heedless of all the cares and concerns of the world. Let the things of the world happen as they may, but you should keep your heart and attention engaged with the Almighty, the Creator of everything. Let not the world and the worldly things affect the innermost soul though you might live in the world and take your share out of it, allotted to you by the Deviser of everything.[2] It was to keep off the worldly cares and useless worries, that shake one's mental poise without bringing about any change in the

---

1 Rūmī : Mathnawī, Book I :

« آب در کشتی هلاک کشتی است   آب اندر زیر کشتی پشتی است »

2 Mujaddid Aḥmad Sirhindī : Letters, Vol. II. Letter 38.

inevitable, that the doctrine of fate was introduced by Islām.[1] It was to keep the mind free for divine meditations that Islām emphasised resignation. Suffice it to say that fate according to Islām is simply another name for the Will of God, and for His will there can be no question of why and how. He possesses full power to do whatever He likes and none dare dispute what He does. Fate is not something unalterable as it is commonly supposed to be, but He Who has fixed it can alter it in any way and at any time He wishes,[3] only that it cannot be altered by anybody else.[1] Islām does not deny the power of God to alter His decree, but what it denies is simply the possibility of its alteration by any power other than that of God.

The kind of asceticism that we are discussing is fatalism in this sense. It emphasises that worldly happenings which occur independently of the control of our will should not engage our attention. We should care only for those things which we can control and such things are of moral and spiritual nature. Therefore, we should live in the world, face its responsibilities and meet its difficulties without allowing these things to take possession of the soul within us. Let our body be busy with its environment and our soul with things divine. This kind of asceticism does not object to the possession of worldly goods even of great value,

1 The Qur'ān LVII. 22-23. 2 *Ibid.* XIII. 39.

3 *Ibid.* XIII. 41.

but what it objects to is to become engrossed in them, that is, to become materialised in thought and secular in outlook, as Rūmī has said, " What is the world? to become careless of God. It does not consist in (the possession of) goods, wealth, wife and children."[1]

I have pointed out above that this kind of asceticism looks like a paradox. A Persian poet has well expressed the paradox involved in this kind of ascetic attitude by saying, " O Lord, Thou hast thrown me in the mid sea with a small plank to float me, then Thou orderest me to be careful and not to wet my skirt in the water."[2] Farīdu'd-dīn 'Aṭṭār has also expressed a similar idea in his Mathnawī.[3]

This kind of attitude can be illustrated by a historical anecdote which is so often quoted by writers on mysticism. One great Sufi known by the name of Ibrāhīm Adham used to travel with great pomp and splendour and with a large retinue of servants, and his tents were pitched with golden pegs. One day a wandering dervish happened to pass by his tents and was extremely surprised to

---

1 Rūmī : Mathnawī, Book I:

« چیست دنیا؟ از خدا غافل بدن   نی قماش و نقره و فرزند و زن »

2 درمیان قعر دریا تخته بندم کرده

بازمیگوئی که دامن ترمکن هشیارباش

3 Farīdu'd-dīn 'Aṭṭār: Mathnawī Ilāhī Nāmah; Nawalkishore Press:

همی گویند در آبم نشانده   که هرگز تر مشو ای باز مانده

مشو تر گرچه در آبی همیشه   در این معرض چه سنجد شیر بیشه

learn that all those things of luxury were owned by one who was once a king and now a Sufi. The dervish with a begging cup in his hand approached the kindly Sufi and said, " It is strange you call yourself a Sufi and still own so much of worldly goods, and thy tents are fixed with golden pegs." He bade the dervish take a little rest, and after an hour or so invited him to travel to Mecca in his company. The dervish agreed. The princely Sufi started for the pilgrimage with the dervish, leaving all his tents and retinue behind. They had not gone far when the dervish remembered that he had forgotten his wooden cup in the tent and requested him to allow him to go back to fetch it. The Sufi then remarked, " This is just the difference between us two: I could afford to part with all my valuables without the least mental worry, while you could not part with a cup of practically no value, without much inconvenience. Those golden pegs which so much surprised you were driven in the earth and not in my heart."[1]

The last sentence of the Sufi well illustrates the asceticism which Islām intended to promulgate, as opposed to the monasticism of Christians, Mendicantism of Buddhists or Rishism of Brahmans. It can thus be summed up, " Be with God with your spirit, mind and heart, and be in the world

---

1 This story is also associated with different names but is very well known among the Sufis.

with your body and hands. Breathe in the air of this world through the nostrils that lead to the lungs and breathe in the air divine through the organs of thy soul that lead thy spirit to the heights above to Allāh, the Almighty Creator."

The superiority of this kind of asceticism over the cruder forms discussed above is clear and unquestionable. It is not suicidal. It does not make a hell of society. It does not allow a seeker of truth to shrink from the responsibilities of life. It does not ask us to shun society or make each person a self-centred entity independent of all social relationships. It only changes the angle of vision, and thus gives a new direction to our activities.

It was this ascetic side in the life and teachings of the founder of Islām which suggested the development of mystic practices among the Muslims. However, this form of asceticism has little in common with its later appearances. In our treatment of the subject we shall try to find out how it lost its original character and assumed new forms. But before we proceed further, we will show that this departure from the practices of the prophet at any rate did not take place in the days of the companions of the prophet.

CHAPTER III.

SUFI TENDENCIES OF THE COMPANIONS OF THE PROPHET.

In all their actions, their ideas, their interpretations of the Law, and their solutions of the various difficult problems of life, the companions totally submitted themselves to the Word of God and completely followed the example of the prophet if any relevant tradition regarding it was available. Whenever they were confronted with a difficult situation they always first searched for an injunction of the Qur'ān to solve it, failing which they relied upon an example or a precept of the prophet applicable to the situation. If neither of these sources helped them, they used their own judgment which in most cases was quite in keeping with the spirit of the Law if not necessarily satisfying the letter of the Sharī'ah. They always acted according to the injunction of the Qur'ān, "If you quarrel about any thing, refer it to Allāh and the Apostle (for decision)."[1] If any one could support his contention with some saying or an example of the prophet related to a similar situation, they accepted the precept literally, otherwise the leader among them gave his judgment according to his personal insight and all accepted that decision.[2]

---

1 The Qur'ān IV. 59.

2 Macdonald: Muslim Theology, pp. 71-72.

So far as asceticism in the Islāmic sense is concerned, the companions were all more or less ascetics. Anecdotes from their biographies can be freely quoted to support the assertion that they did not care much for the worldly goods. It is related about Abū Bakr, the first Caliph, that on one occasion when asked by the prophet to contribute towards some charitable fund, he brought down all his worldly possessions and handed them over to him. When asked by the prophet whether he had left anything for his family members, he replied that he had left them in the care of Allāh and His Apostle.[1]

Their houses were free from costly furniture. They lived most frugally and did not think of hoarding wealth. They were conscious of the fact that luxurious living destroys the strength of a nation as well as of an individual. It was really this hard living which was the secret of their success in war and peace. 'Umar, the second successor of the prophet, was once found to have been wearing clothes that were stitched in as many as twelve places.[2] His family expenses amounted to two dirhams per day, which is equal to annas ten of our present coinage. They were very generous so far as their helping others was concerned, but they were very frugal in their personal expenses.

---

1 Tirmidhī: Ṣaḥih XLVI. 16; Cairo 1292.

2 Shiblī: Al-Farūq, p. 141.

It is related about Ḥasan, one of the grandsons of the prophet, that once his servant inadvertently threw a boiling dish of soup on his master. Thinking that he would be severely punished for it, he repeated the verse of the Qur'ān, "Those who restrain their anger......"[1] Ḥasan said he was not angry. "And pardon men," added the servant. Ḥasan said, "I pardon you." "And Allāh loves the doers of good," concluded the offending slave. "I give you liberty and four hundred pieces of silver," was the response.[2] Sale comments upon this incident by saying, "A noble instance of moderation and generosity."

They spent their days in serving the cause of Islām, either in the battlefield, or in the courts of justice, or in working out the schemes of administration, and spent their nights and mornings in prayer. Their biographies clearly show us that it is not luxury that commands respect but discipline and hard work in the service of humanity. They were conscious of the truth that only certain moral, social and spiritual qualities were all that were required for fighting out the battle of life.

They did not habitually indulge in abstract ideas. They were essentially men of action. With the exception of a few fragmentary poetic compositions none of them is known to have written any systematic literary work, nor could they afford

1 The Qur'ān III: 133.

2 M. Muḥammad Ali: Translation of the Qur'ān, note 492.

time to do so, as in the beginning all their energies were concentrated on merely defending their existence, and later on expanding the bounds of Islām. They considered the Qur'ān to be enough for their guidance and their literary instincts were all directed towards its understanding and interpretation. They had no independent view of life except the one which they had learnt from the prophet. Nor did they frame any theories on the problems of the universe; they faithfully tried to follow their master in word and deed.

Their biographies have come down to us as much intact as that of the prophet. The reason is that the early Muslim traditionists who were the pioneers of Muslim history considered it a great sin to exaggerate or to circulate any false report about any person. These traditionists were so deeply convinced of the truth of the mission of the prophet, of the righteousness of the companions and of the ultimate triumph of the truth, that there was no necessity of falsifying the record of anybody's life. Moreover, the early Muslim traditionists were also conscious of the fact that it was the exaggerated and uncritically recorded reports about the lives of the founders of various religions that were responsible for introducing mythology and polytheism in those revealed religions.

The result was that the Muslim traditionists developed a historical method of criticism which has not been equalled in strictness and rigour by the rules of any historical enquiry. They devised definite rules for testing and judging the truthfulness or falsehood of any report alleged to have been connected with the life of the prophet or of any one of his companions. Search as carefully as you like the biographies and the histories of pre-Islāmic days, they will be found with rare exceptions full of myths and exaggerations that can hardly be believed.[1] This holds true without exception at least with regard to the sacred biographies of different founders of prevalent religions.

Unfortunately the biographies of many saints of Islām, particularly of later days, are full of exaggerations and mythology. A cursory glance over the biographies of pre-Islāmic days will convince the reader that all this has crept in

---

1 Herodotus, Thucydides and Livy are the most outstanding names among the ancient Greeks and Romans, that deserve to be called historians in any sense. Herodotus was criticised by Thucydides for his inaccuracy. Thucydides though having more critical sense is considered to be unauthentic for putting speeches in the mouths of his heroes, which he never could have ascertained by first hand evidence. Livy is considered to be unreliable because he was ever anxious to guard the honour of Rome. Thus in many places he introduced his own notions of what could be expected from a Roman; rather than giving a fair account of actual occurrences. This makes him unfair, one-sided and unreliable. None of them ever enunciated the principles on the basis of which the value of historical records could be judged. This was done for the first time by the Muslim Traditionists.

See the introductions to Ibn Mājā, Dārimī, and Tirmidhī.

See the Ancient Greek historians by Bury (Macmillan Press).

Cf. Encyclopædia Britannica, 13th Edition, on Thucydides and Livy.

owing to the introduction of the non-Islāmic elements among the Muslims, which did incalculable harm to their simple morality. Many stories of miraculous performances of the pre-Islāmic personages have been anachronised and associated with the name of Muslim saints. Credulous Muslims tried to follow the Persian and Christian literatures that had come down to them.[1] So long as Islām was free from the influence of such literatures, it was also free from all mythology and exaggeration, and it was regarded as an unpardonable sin to report any false occurrence as true, as was done by Christian missionaries in the name of church and saints for centuries together. The prophet is reported to have said, "May I tell you what are the greatest of great sins; to worship any one other than the One Allāh, to disobey one's parents, and to concoct false evidence (to report a false story)."[2] Accordingly, the early traditionists very severely tested every statement made about the prophet or his companions. It is on account of this fact, that the life accounts of the prophet and his companions have come down to us without the least exaggeration.

All reports about the companions agree that in spite of their austerity of life they were social.

---

1 See Siyaru'l-Aqṭāb in Persian. It purports to be a brief history of the famous saints of Chishtī order. It is full of foul exaggerations about most members of the order. (Imperial Library, Calcutta. Oriental Section.)

2 Bukhārī: Ṣaḥiḥ, Kitābu' Shādāt.

They said their obligatory prayers in the mosque and took interest in every social function. Society for them was not a convenient name for play, enjoyment and pleasure; they understood it to be a medium and a means which offered them opportunities for doing their duties towards God and towards humanity at large. They tried to practise all the social virtues that are described in the Qur'ān or Ḥadith. Almost all the cardinal principles of Islām, saying prayers five times in the common place of worship, payment of poor-tax and going to Mecca once in life are more or less intended to be performed in society and for the betterment of society. They realised this social principle underlying the Islāmic institutions and tried to act up to them.

This public performance of religious ceremonies had made their social life completely harmonious and this fact was not a little responsible for their success and achievement. It had developed in them a unity of purpose. The ideals that were placed before them by the precept and example of the prophet were intended to be common for all the Muslims. This community of ideals combined with their social virtues had created among them the unity of purpose and the unity of action. In short, they all desired the same thing, worked for the same thing, in one and the same way. The success of their undertakings was the sure consequence of this kind of unity.

The prophet was ordered by God to consult the faithful.[1] Similarly every one among the companions considered it to be his duty to consult his brethren in faith in important matters. The Qur'ān refers to this virtue of the companions when it says, "Their rule (of life) is to take counsel among themselves."[2] Thus by consultation among themselves they devised a common path, on which they marched unitedly with a single plan of action, previously decided among themselves.

They always helped one another, but for the sake of good and not for the sake of evil, for the Qur'ān had enjoined, "Help one another in goodness and piety, and do not help one another in sin and aggression."[3]

This social disposition was a cure for the evil consequences of their asceticism if they practised any. When, later Sufis gave up these social practices, and confined themselves to monasteries, the Christian and Buddhistic asceticism found its way among the Sufi circles, and the natural result was the destruction and dissolution of Muslim society, at least so far as the influence of the Sufis was concerned. The disappearance of cardinal Islāmic virtues from among the Sufis marks the degradation of their society as a class.

1 The Qur'ān III. 158. 2 *Ibid.* XII. 38.
3 *Ibid.* V. 2.

The companions interpreted the Qur'ān as the prophet had explained to them. They did not touch the mystic and controversial verses. They acted according to the verse of the Qur'ān which lays down, "He it is who has revealed the Book to you: some of its verses are decisive, they are the basis of the Book and the others are allegorical; those in whose heart there is perversity (disease) they follow that part of it which is allegorical, seeking to mislead, and seeking to give it (their own) interpretation; but none knows its interpretation except Allāh; and those who are firmly rooted in knowledge they say: We believe in it, it is all from our Lord."[1] The companions acted according to the plain verses of the Qur'ān and the clear dictates of Islām, and did not touch the controversial verses. But in later days this order was reversed, and the learned doctors and famous Sufis discussed the controversial points only, without paying much regard to the clear injunctions of the Qur'ān.

The companions as a class kept aloof from all such controversies and discussions. They clearly realised that salvation could be attained by means of good actions and not by means of good discussions. Moreover, they had hardly any time left to indulge in abstruse hair-splitting, which was highly developed by the Greeks when the Greek society was disintegrating and which developed among the Muslims when Greek philosophy influenced their

---

1 The Qur'ān III. 6.

literature and society at a later age.

Discussions and controversies as a means of spreading truth, except on rare occasions, are of little value. The biographies of the prophets who came with a definite mission support this assertion. It is the force of assertion that convinces. It is the mental zeal of the preacher that converts and not the force of the contestant's arguments. "Believe and thou shalt learn" is the true exposition of human mentality rather than "Discuss and thou shalt be convinced".

Discussion instead of clearing up the difficulties strengthens the prejudices of the disputants, thus making the understanding of the question at issue impossible. In the end it usually leaves each disputant more strongly confirmed in his own opinion. Moreover, since it places both the parties on the same level it makes the conviction difficult. Each one thinks himself equal to another and thus equally authorised to continue and prolong the discussion, for there can be no end of the possibilities of any kind of knowledge, nor any dearth of reasons to support any kind of inferences.

It may be pointed out that though conviction may not result from discussion, yet it is the only possible way of the exposition of truth. It may also be pointed out that it is highly undesirable to discuss for the sake of discussion alone. Its object should always be to elicit truth, and therefore, a discussion started with this object in mind is highly commendable.

Islām had clearly realised that discussions do not make conversions. The Qur'ān therefore enjoined upon the prophet and the faithful on numerous occasions not to waste their time in discussing the truth with those who discuss only for the sake of creating confusion and who can never discuss about anything but in the light of their pre-conceived false notions. As it is impossible for such persons to benefit from discussions or to arrive at any truth, it is mere waste of time to argue things with them. Just to quote one Qur'ānic verse out of innumerable ones on the same point, " Surely those who disbelieve, it being alike to them whether you warn them or do not warn them, will not believe; Allāh has set a seal upon their hearts, and their hearing, and there is a covering over their eyes and there is a great chastisement for them."[1] A great deal has been said about this seal of Allāh by numerous commentators of the Qur'ān as well as by its critics. Really speaking this seal is nothing but their mental prejudices and pre-conceptions which have closed the door of knowledge and progress to them. They have heard certain things from their forefathers and have seen them performing certain acts of devotion to gods and deities, and have learnt certain ideas of divinity and religion from them, and now when the apostle of Allāh who has come with the truth

1 The Qur'ān II. 6, 7.

wants to convey certain new and greater truths about Allāh, His Angels, His Attributes, and His Creation, their pre-conceptions and prejudices do not allow them to hear, see, or understand his teachings, thus precluding them from the apprehension of higher and nobler truths. It is this seal of their preconceived prejudices which has deafened their ears, blinded their eyes, and choked up their hearts against the sublime truths. It is therefore quite useless to discuss and argue with such people. They can never be guided aright unless they give up their hereditary notions, their idols of the den and of the tribe.

The Qur'ān, further, does not encourage personal references. It has referred to many discussions between historical personalities and has sometimes even referred to the details of such discussions, but the God-fearing party in such disputes is usually shown to avoid personal references. Moreover, the Qur'ān always clearly defines the point at issue, and lays it down barely before its opponents, challenging them to refute its arguments if they can. Thus we see that Islām has generally discouraged useless and irritative discussions although it has recommended healthy discussions for the investigation of truth.[1]

Here is an illustration of this principle. The Qur'ān in challenging the followers of the

1 The Qur'ān XVI. 125.

previous revealed books, invites them to accept first the fundamental principles which are common to both Islām and their religion, and then proceeds to discuss the minor details specially referring to the doctrines of their faith as stated in their respective books. It says, "Say, O followers of the Book! Come to an equitable agreement between us and you that we shall not serve any but Allāh, and that we shall not associate aught with Him, and that some of us shall not take others for lords besides Allāh."[1] With regard to the unbelievers, who do not agree with Islām even about the fundamental principles, the Qur'ān lays down, "O prophet! strive hard (dispute hard) against the unbelievers and the hypocrites; and be hard with them."[2] Since there is no common principle between the belief of the polytheists and Islām, the Qur'ān in order to convince such opponents draws its arguments chiefly from the sources of natural phenomena and sensible things which can be commonly observed by all human beings alike. It is clear, therefore, that the Qur'ān starts in all discussions with commonly agreed principles, strictly excludes all irrelevant points and consciously limits all its arguments to clearly defined questions. It never loses sight of the points to be proved and it follows the most praiseworthy method of repeating the fundamental question at issue after stating some points of argument. This point has often

1 The Qur'ān III, 63. 2 *Ibid.* IX. 73.

been criticised by the ignorant as useless repetition, but the truth is that this method of repeatedly referring to the fundamental questions at issue and thus keeping before the mind of the reader a clear vision of the object of discussion, adds not only to the charm and beauty of the language, but also to the convincing power of the Book. If you analyse the speech of an orator and try to find out which of his assertions have impressed you most, you will always find that those sentences, which he could nicely repeat in different forms and in excellently arranged contexts, have convinced you most. The ancient art of rhetorics consisted in repeating the ideas in various forms in order to carry conviction to the audience. Therefore, in order to convince the hearers and to create an impression on them, which is the primary object of the Qur'ān, a certain amount of repetition in different forms and in different contexts was essential and indispensable.

So far, we have considered the value of discussions and controversies for the purpose of carrying conviction. Another method of arriving at truth, which is more or less opposed to discussions, is that of accepting it from authority. It is essential, on this account, that we should now try to judge the value of authority, from the Islāmic point of view. This question is very important on other considerations as well, for it is on this basis, that different sects have been formed among the Muslims.

Without entering into the merits or demerits of

any sect we can say that their difference lies not in their belief or disbelief in authority abstractly, but in the authority of this person or that person, over and above a common belief in the authority of the Qur'ān and the prophet. In the absolute authority of these two all sects of Islām agree. Therefore, authority of some kind is indispensable from the point of view of every sect. We shall discuss here the value of authority for the purposes of conviction, as opposed to discussions and controversies. In order to avoid sectarian controversies we shall limit ourselves to the question of authority in general.

Authority, as opposed to discussion, hardly ever fails to convince. As ordinarily understood it is the subjection of one's will to that of another. Conviction is that state of our cognition at which the cognition is about to be transferred into volition. It is a state of mind in which will is about to preponderate over the other mental elements. This statement becomes clear when we consider that conviction is usually followed by an action. Consequently, the stronger and freer from doubt the conviction is, the stronger will be its crystallisation into action. As will accepts the judgment of authority most readily so the conviction must be strongest when coming from an authority. This fact is supported by our experience of every day life. If the teacher of a student asks him to study a particular book on a particular subject, he will accept the suggestion more readily than if it were to come from a fellow student, provided he does not think as highly of his friend as of his teacher. A soldier accepts the command of his officer and immediately proceeds to obey him without any question or discussion. Conviction, therefore, is a belief brought about by the superior will of a higher personality, which one holds in respect. It is because of this aspect of human nature that the prophets always first tried to establish the superiority of the will of God and of their own over the will of other human beings. In the Qur'ān, Noaḥ, Hūd, Ṣāliḥ and Shu'ayb are all made to say, "Surely I am a faithful apostle of Allāh: therefore be afraid of Allāh and obey me."[1]

Authority is the best means of educating and reforming the character. Why is so much importance attached to good laws as a means of reforming the individuals composing the society? I think for no other reason than that it is implied that laws as coming from a superior authority must be obeyed and as such must succeed in reforming the life of the members of the society for which they are framed. It is true that sometimes the laws are also affected and moulded by the customs and the morals of the persons composing the society, but that also happens because the will of the members is collectively accepted as a superior authority for that purpose.

1 The Qur'ān XXVI. 107-179.

Why is discipline considered to be the best way of preparing for the struggle of life? Simply because it is enforced by a superior authority either by the higher principle of one's own nature, that is by reason, or by that of another who is accepted as possessing a more forceful will than one's own.

Why is example considered to be better than precept? Simply because the former, coming from the superior personality or from any personality so considered by us, convinces and impresses us more strongly than a mere precept which involves only an intellectual perception, which as such does not necessarily carry with it the conviction of the superiority of the will of the person from whom it comes.

Another reason why authority is convincing is that we are born and brought up under its care. Since the very time of our birth every moment of our life is spent in imitating others, and in learning from them. Up to a particular stage we are required to obey them blindly, without questioning the *rational* of their orders. Nor are we at this stage fit to question and criticize the conduct or the command of those who decidedly possess a will superior to that of ours. A little later comes the stage when, still obeying the authority, we can choose between different authorities and can prefer one to the others. In matters of education we begin to prefer the authority of our teachers over that of our comparatively less learned parents. In matters of religion we begin to prefer the opinion of theologians and specialists to that of others. In this way we begin to distinguish between the authority of specialists and amateurs pertaining to any branch of human knowledge or human activity. It goes without saying, that at the later stage of life the capacity to choose the right authority at the right time and to follow it rightly in action, contributes a good deal to making life a success and to coming out victorious in the struggle of existence.

Last of all comes the stage of emancipation. At this stage we still obey authority, not as such, but rather as a principle which we have ourselves judged to be superior. In the case of a large number of persons this third stage of complete emancipation from authority is hardly ever achieved during their life time. There are others for whom this stage hardly proves to be happy because they enter into it without preparation enough to guard against its evil effects. Such people, indeed, are less happy than those who simply content themselves with selecting the best authority as their guide for action. But there is no doubt that the small number of persons, who cross the first two stages successfully and enter into the third stage with sufficient preparation, render greater service to humanity and to the world at large than the whole lot of human beings in the first and the second stages taken together, as the saying goes, "Many claim but few are chosen."

Those chosen few, who cross the limits of obedience to authority, are those geniuses who decide the destinies of nations and countries on this sphere. History affords a number of instances of such geniuses who have controlled the destiny of this sphere in the different epochs of its history. After a period, these persons themselves become an immutable authority. Often they are deified. With one stroke of their genius they add as much to the glory of this world as average men all combined together could hardly achieve within centuries. They extend the horizon of life. They offer a new explanation of life, and place new ideals before humanity. They change its direction, give it a new turn, and, so to speak, pull it upwards.

Such a personality is a blessing for the world, but with certain reservations. As misdirected energy can destroy existing things rather than create new ones, similarly a misguided genius can cause a greater harm to the progress and peace of the world than a very large number of misguided persons belonging to the first or the second stage. A number of historical personages can be quoted to support this statement. Abū Jahl, Abū-Lahab, Alexander, Hannibal and Napoleon throughout their life and Khālid b. Walīd and 'Umar Fārūq before their conversion to Islām, were such dangerous personalities. Napoleon, Alexander and Hannibal wasted their whole genius in useless and troublesome wars and bloodshed. When unbelievers, Khālid and 'Umar were deadly enemies of Islām, but under the guidance and authority of the prophet, a much greater and a mightier personality, they turned out to be the shining gems of Islām.

It is very difficult to fix up the line of demarcation between authority and independence, that is, it is very difficult to settle finally how far one must obey authority and beyond what limit one can act and think independently. In solving this difficulty Islām has adopted the most rational media. For ordinary Muslims, who on account of their worldly pursuits can hardly spare time for specialisation in theology, it offers authority as the rule of life. It does not encourage such persons to theorise or analogize in the domain of religion. But even such persons are not totally deprived of using independent judgment.

This independence of thought is granted to common persons in two ways. Firstly, Islām lays down a minima and a maxima, the two extreme limits within which they can exercise their independent will and within which they can choose this or that action.[1] They are not encouraged to pass judgments upon the actions and opinions of others, inasmuch as they have not crossed the second stage of submission to authority, and consequently their views cannot be accepted in the interests of society in general. Secondly, the number of authorities has been limited in the case of ordinary Muslims. In religious obser-

---

1 The Qur'ān II. 229.

vances, they need not follow the authority or any and every body, may he be a saint or a reputed theologian. If they follow every theologian indiscriminately, then their independent spirit would be totally crushed, and once it happens they will not be able to progress spiritually, which is the chief object of Islām. Therefore, Islām has limited their obedience to the authority of the prophet alone. In any matter of religion when they come to know that the prophet said or acted in a particular way, they need not search for any other light or guidance. Thirdly, Islām has enjoined upon every Muslim to weigh and judge every opinion in the light of the commands clearly laid down by Allāh and His Apostle. The Qur'ān explicitly lays down this principle by saying, "O you who believe! obey Allāh and obey the Apostle, and those in authority from among you; then if you quarrel about anything, refer it to Allāh and the Apostle (*i.e.*, to the Qur'ān and Traditions)".[1] In this way Islām fostered a spirit of independence and free-thinking, side by side with the total subjection of one's will to the superior will of Allāh and His Apostle. In this way Islām adjusted the claims of authority and independence for the ordinary Muslims. Beginning with total and blind obedience to authority, as a child begins its life, a Muslim is led to choose freely among different authorities and thence to complete inde-

1 The Qur'ān IV. 59.

pendence of thought.

But as regards those who have passed through the first two stages successfully, Islām allows to take lead in matters religious as well as worldly. Such persons are technically called Mujtahidūn. They rise above the level of average Muslims on account of their better acquaintance with the Law, their deep and thorough study of the Qur'ān and Sunnah, their superior intellect, and their intense love for their Creator and His creatures. In matters of religion they have a right to guide others because they are nearer to the source of goodness, on account of their extraordinary piety and religious knowledge. Such people also become an authority for the faithful, but of a much lower standard than that of the prophet. The Sufis contest that mere love of Allāh and His Apostle can grant this claim of passing judgment upon others, but the learned section of the Muslims has never agreed to this opinion. They contend that free thought unsupported by the Book or Sunnah may lead to the rovings of imagination. Conjecture in matters of religion has been clearly forbidden by the Qur'ān which says, "They do not follow anything but conjecture, and surely conjecture does not avail against the truth at all."[1]

It is not irrelevant to point out here that in the matter of authority also Sufis have failed to

1 The Qur'ān LIII. 28.

adopt the view of Islām, which, as I have pointed out above, considers the authority of Allāh and His Apostle as the only ultimately binding force. The Sufis as a class consider the authority of their Shaikh in no way less binding than the authority of the prophet. In theory, perhaps, they would agree that they accept their Shaikh only so far as he guides them to Allāh and His prophet, but in actual practice it is difficult to distinguish which of the two, the prophet or the Shaikh, has a greater sway over them.[1] We shall take up this question in detail when we shall examine the famous Sufi theory of different stages of spiritual progress, of annihilation in Shaikh, in prophet and last of all merger into God.

The important point to be ascertained here is how far the authority of the companions of the prophet is binding upon the faithful. The Qur'ān does not usually mention proper names, except those of the historical personages who in some way glorified the name of Allāh. So far as I think even such names are often intended to stand for type of persons, about whom something is to be conveyed, not as individuals, but as representatives of a certain class possessing those prominent characteristics which are associated with that

---

1 An illustration of this kind of blind reliance on Shaikh is found in the famous verse of Ḥāfiẓ of Shīrāz:

به مئے سجاده رنگین کن گرت پیر مغان گوید
که سالك بیخبر نبود ز راه و رسم منزلها

individual name, partly for the sake of convenience, and partly on account of that name being familiar to those who were the first recipients of the prophet's message. The proper names of the previous prophets have been very profusely used, but it is because they represent a *corporation sole*, a series of a class of persons possessing certain rights and certain duties. The Qur'ān has expressed this view by saying, "Surely this is your community: one community (preaching similar doctrines and professing similar faith), and I am your Lord, therefore, serve Me."[1] Similarly, the Qur'ān describes a class of persons who possess certain qualities, which fit in with the character of some of the companions. For instance, the Qur'ān refers to a companion who was accompanying the prophet during his migration to Medina.[2] History tells us that this person was Abū Bakr, the first successor of the prophet, but the Qur'ān does not mention any name. Again on another occasion the Qur'ān enjoins upon the faithful in general terms, not to stop the help that one might have been giving to one's relations for a trifling offence, not connected with the negligence of any cardinal principle or injunction of Islām.[3] History tells us that it refers to an occasion when the same companion had stopped the allowance of his nephew, who had joined the hypocrites in accusing one of the wives

---

1 The Qur'ān XXI. 19. 2 *Ibid.* IX. 40.

3 *Ibid.* XXIV. 22.

of the prophet. Here again the Qur'ān does not mention the name.

Again there are many sayings of the prophet in praise of his different companions. Once he is reported to have said, "My companions are the best of men."[1] He is reported to have said on another occasion, "My companions are like the stars, whomsoever you follow, you will be on the right path."[2] In short, according to a reasonable interpretation of the Qur'ān and Sunnah the authority of the companions is an established principle,[3] only that it is next in importance to the authority of the prophet. Whenever, therefore, any interpretation of an Islāmic doctrine can be traced back to the companions it should be accepted as an authoritative interpretation. They had lived with the prophet and had always tried to mould their actions, views and opinions according to those of the prophet; therefore, next to the prophet they can be accepted as a most reliable authority in all matters of religion. There is no historical evidence to support that they or any one of them ever tried to lay the foundation of a new path other than that laid down by the prophet, and we can say with more or less certainty that after they had received light and guidance

---

1 Aḥmed b. Ḥanbal: Musnad I. 379. ed. Cairo, 1313.

2 Ṭaysīru'l Wuṣūl. Vol. III, p. 260 (Cairo 1346 A.H.) where it is given on the dubious authority of Razīn, known as Ibnu'l-'Abdarī.

3 Dārimī: Intr. b. 19, ed. Dehli 1337.

from the prophet they should have been the last persons to do this. They are known to have transmitted everything which they received from the prophet faithfully to their posterity, nor are they known to have ever claimed to have received any secret teachings from the prophet apart from the teachings of the Law, the Book and the Sunnah. The story that the prophet taught secret knowledge to 'Alī or to any one else among his companions shall be discussed in the next chapter.

Since the companions tried to follow the prophet in everything, their practices also betray a tendency towards mysticism and asceticism, but they did not develop it as a theory of life. They did not believe it to be a principle of reclusion and mendicancy. They were highly social, but cared little for the worldly goods. They possessed only so much of worldly goods as was just enough to satisfy their bare necessaries of life. They lived a life as austere, probably more austere than that of those persons who had begun to live in seclusion later. They were a source of comfort for others but did not expect others to serve them. It is reported that while taking the oath of allegiance, the prophet, among other things, enjoined upon the new converts not to request others for anything. The early companions were so strict in this matter, that if while riding, any one happened to drop his whip, he personally got down to pick it, and would not ask others to pick it up for him.[1] This is the real spirit of democracy and personal independence. It is said about Caliph 'Umar I that when he was proceeding towards Syria to take charge of the city of Jerusalem where the victorious Arab armies were waiting for his arrival, he and his servant had only one camel to ride. One camel could not accommodate both of them along with provisions for the way. He, therefore, agreed with his servant to ride and tie. When they arrived near the conquered city it was the turn of the servant to ride the camel. The Caliph, the elected leader of the whole Muslim community, whose representative armies had been conquering the big towns of Persia and Syria, entered the holy city of Jerusalem, with the halter of the camel in his hand and the servant seated on its back. He knew that he had come there to take charge of one of the most famous cities of the world, famous for its religious and historical associations, but this did not deter him in the least from discharging his moral obligation, voluntarily accepted by himself, of giving his servant his due. In this way the companions of the prophet acted up to the principles of equality and justice. In short they lived a true Islāmic life for which the prophet had himself laid down a precedent.

Just like the prophet they spent their day in earning their livelihood and in fighting for their

1 Ṭaysīru'l Wuṣūl: Vol. I, p. 22 (Cairo, 1346).

defence, and their night in praying to their Almighty Creator. But prayers in the form of Dhikr as now prevalent among the Sufis were unknown to them. They believed more in silent musings, silently muttering the names of Allāh, in performing their duties according to the clear dictates of Islām, and not jumping, howling and barking as certain sects of Sufis do while performing their Dhikr,[1] which they believe to have been enjoined upon them by the founders of their respective orders. Such practices can be traced to have existed among certain religious orders of unbelievers even in the days of the prophet himself. The Qur'ān severely criticises such sects as make a joke and a play of their religion.[2] Those people who sing and whistle at the time of performing their religious prayers are accused of ignorance and folly by the Qur'ān.[3] Islām takes a serious view of life. It expects that at least that phase of human life which is connected with the worship of God, with spiritual development and with moral ideals must be regarded as serious and must be taken up in a serious mood. No such action should be done at the time of praying to Almighty God that might smack of light-heartedness. Islām favours a mental attitude midway between the two moods of jocoseness and moroseness. While making the toils of life lighter, it does not want to make life a childish play. Our experience

1 Brown : Dervishes and Oriental Spiritualists.

2 The Qur'ān II. 231. 3 *Ibid.* VIII. 35.

of light-hearted persons in our daily life is not very happy. It cannot be otherwise, since want of seriousness creates a mental attitude of irresponsibility and carelessness. Irresponsible persons become indifferent to the good of others and this indifference can hardly be distinguished at least in its net effect from the devil-may-care and light-hearted nature.

It is clear, therefore, that such practices as of dancing and howling could not have been originated by the founders of their respective orders. Some of them are an outcome of human nature's love for innovation; some others owe their existence to the love of unhealthy asceticism; while the rest can be traced, as already pointed out, to the influence of foreign mystics. We fail to find any trace of such mystic rites and practices among the companions.

The next point that we wish to ascertain is how far these rites can be connected with the first and early founders of the Sufi sects among the Muslims. We shall, therefore, try to find out how far any one of these founders was responsible for the practices prevalent among the present day Sufis. We shall further examine some of the prevalent doctrines which pass as fundamentals of Sufism.

CHAPTER IV.

ṬARĪQAH AND SHARĪʿAH.

"Indeed, Allāh conferred a benefit upon the believers when He raised among them an Apostle from among themselves, reciting to them His communications and purifying them and teaching them the Book and the Wisdom,"[1] says the Qur'ān. The Sufis says that the term Kitāb and Ḥikmah in this context mean Sharīʿah and Ṭarīqah respectively. They say that the mission of the prophet was two-fold, one to teach the knowledge of the Book which they call Sharīʿah or ʿIlmu'ẓ-Ẓāhir, and the second to teach Ḥikmah or Ṭarīqah, which is called ʿIlmu'l-Bāṭin. To teach the first kind of knowledge had been the mission of every prophet but to teach Ḥikmah along with it was the special mission of the prophet of Islām.

The second kind of teaching, the Sufis say, he could not impart openly, since every man could not easily grasp its intricate and knotty problems. This esoteric teaching, therefore, he secretly conveyed to his more advanced followers, particularly to his cousin and son-in-law ʿAlī. This system of teaching has been called ʿIlmu'l-Bāṭin, firstly because it is connected with the development of the spirit or soul which is the hidden

1 The Qur'ān III. 163. Cf. LII. 2.

essence of our organism, secondly because the prophet taught it secretly to his cousin, and thirdly because at a later stage of Islāmic history it was associated with the name of a class of reactionaries, the Bāṭinites (the esoterists), who under the influence of Persian nationalism, Greek philosophy and neo-Platonic ideals began to attach a great deal of importance to it.[1]

'Ilmu'z-Ẓāhir (exoteric knowledge), say the Sufis, was openly preached by the prophet in the Kitāb (the Qur'ān) or Sunnah (Traditions) and was more closely connected with the social, economical, political, juristical and ethical aspects of our life, whereas 'Ilmu'l-Bāṭin was said to concern our spiritual development.

In order to support all this an anecdote is related from the life of the prophet, according to which on the day of the battle of Tā'if, he is reported to have conversed with 'Alī for a very long time.[2] The Sufis assert that since there was no secrecy about the clear orders and laws of Sharī'ah, this conversation must have been about Ṭarīqah, the Path, or 'Ilmu'l-Bāṭin.

Such a conclusion, when carefully examined, turns out to be unfounded. The anecdote about the secret conversation above referred to is altogether unauthentic and cannot be supported by historical

---

1 Macdonald: Muslim Theology, p. 42.

2 Farīdu'd-dīn Aṭṭār: Mathnawī, Jawharu'dh-Dhāt, Vol. I, p. 135.

evidence. But even if it be true it does not at all justify the conclusion that it was connected with the teachings of the secret mission or Ṭarīqah by the prophet. 'Alī was the cousin and son-in-law of the prophet and probably the nearest relation among his companions. It is very likely that the prophet may have consulted him or conveyed to him anything about his own or his daughter's household affairs. Evidently, the prophet could not be expected to have talked about such domestic affairs publicly in the presence of all his companions.

Moreover, there were many other companions of the prophet about whom the Muslims agree, as a community, that they were in no way inferior to 'Alī spiritually or intellectually. Therefore, there could be no reason for the prophet to have kept these things secret from them. No such secret conversation of the prophet with anyone of them is reported. The story further connects Ḥasan of Baṣra to be the receiver of this secret knowledge from 'Alī. Ḥasan-al-Basri was only nineteen years old at the time of 'Alī's death and was brought up at Baṣra.[1] It is highly improbable, therefore, that he should have been entrusted with the propagation of the mystic doctrine at such a young age. The story seems to have acquired plausibility on account of his pro-Fāṭimide leanings. Indeed if we do not connect the descendents of 'Alī as interposing links, the doctrine of Ṭarīqah cannot at all be proved to have emanated

1 Encyclopædia of Islam, Vol. II, on al-Ḥasan of Baṣra.

from the prophet. Search history as much as you like, no trace of any such secret knowledge can be connected even with the sayings of any one of the immediate descendents of 'Alī, till very late when it can be traced to other sources and other causes and influences more directly connected with it. It is impossible, therefore, to ascertain its connection with any saying of any one of the companions.

Again there is no indication in the Qur'ān or Traditions to support the view that the mission of the prophet was two-fold. The Qur'ān clearly lays down that the mission of the prophet was the same with which the other prophets were sent prior to him. The Qur'ān says, "Surely We have revealed to you as We revealed to Noaḥ and the prophets after him, and We revealed to Abraham and Ishmael and Isaac and Jacob and the tribes, and Jesus and Job and Jonah and Aaron and Solomon and We gave to David a scripture."[1] Again, the Qur'ān considers all the prophets as belonging to one community, delivering the same messages, teaching almost the same doctrines, and performing the same acts. After relating the account of different prophets, the Qur'ān lays down, "Verily your community is one community (preaching similar doctrines and professing similar faith) and I am your Lord, therefore, serve Me."[2] The Qur'ān expresses the same idea more strongly by saying, "Naught is said (revealed) to you but what was said (revealed)

1 The Qur'ān IV. 163. 2 *Ibid.* XXI. 92.

to the apostles before you."[1] In another context it is repeated still more clearly, "Thus does Allāh, the Mighty, the Wise, reveal to you and (thus did He reveal) to those before you."[2] Thus, it is quite clear that the Qur'ān does not in any way support the theory that the mission of the prophet of Islām was two-fold, as different from the mission of the previous prophets who came with one mission only. It disapproves the practice of making a distinction among different apostles to the detriment of one or the other.[3] The prophet did not like to be extolled over other prophets and when he heard somebody doing it in his presence, he always rebuked him for doing it.[4]

We should next examine how far the interpretation of the Sufis of the Qur'ānic verse referring to Kitāb and Ḥikmah is reasonable. Different sects and their representative writers have differently interpreted the term Ḥikmah in the above context. Some say that the Kitāb means the Qur'ān while Ḥikmah refers to the Sunnah or Traditions. Some other writers, like Wali'ullāh Muḥaddith, of Delhi say that the term Ḥikmah means nice logical reasons that have been adduced in the Qur'ān to support its fundamental doctrines.[5] In support of their interpretation they offer verses

1 The Qu'rān XLI. 43. 2 *Ibid.* XLII. 3. 3 *Ibid.* II. 285.
4 Muslim : Ṣaḥīḥ, Faḍā'il t. 163 ; cf. Bukhārī : Ṣaḥīḥ, Tafsīru'l Qur'ān.
Ḥujjatu'llāhi'l Bālighah, first two chapters.

like this, "We reveal of the Qur'ān that which is a healing and a mercy to the believers."[1] They think that 'healing' refers to that portion of the Qur'ān which relates to the laws and commands of the nature of "Must", while mercy refers to that portion which supports the fundamental doctrines of faith like the Unity and Existence of God, prophethood, resurrection in the next world, and many other similar ones on logical grounds. The Sufis, as has been already pointed out above, interpret the term wisdom in the sense of Ṭarīqah.

It is in itself a strong objection to the interpretation of Sufis, that Ḥikmah could have been taught by the prophet secretly, only to a chosen few. For, if it was a truth it ought to have been taught openly to all and sundry. Further there is no evidence that the prophet ever talked any truth secretly to any one. Indeed it is inconceivable that he should have kept any truths secret. If there were really any truths which he did not disclose to all, then it would show that he had left certain truths untold and certain secrets unrevealed, which would mean that he did not discharge his mission rightly. But this is unbelievable in the light of other facts known through the historical evidence regarding his discharge of the mission with which he was sent to human beings.[2] The prophet is reported to have said, "It

1 The Qur'ān XVII. 82.

2 Bukhārī : Ṣaḥīḥ, Ḥijjatu'l-Widā'; cf. Muslim: Ṣaḥīḥ, Ḥijjatu'n-Nabī ; cf. Mujaddid Aḥmad Sirhindī, Letters Vol. I, p. 272.

is sinful to say that I have concealed anything revealed to me."[1]

Some Sufi writers have not hesitated to say that these doctrines were secretly told to only a few because all could not understand them. They have forgotten that for many even the ordinary fundamentals of Islām with which he had started his mission were not easy to grasp. The Arabs could hardly understand the ideas of resurrection, of the Day of Judgment, of Reward and Punishment, in short of life in any other world excepting this in which we live. The very notion of the Unity of God which is the foundation of all faiths and more particularly that of Islām could not be easily understood by many, as to many even to this day the very notion of the existence of God is not quite intelligible. The theory of prophethood was no less easy to understand. But when all these doctrines were openly and fervently preached by him and in the end almost established by his ceaseless efforts, where lay the difficulty for him in preaching and establishing the greater truths if they were as momentous as the doctrines of the Unity and Resurrection?

If we try to find out the sense in which the term Ḥikmah was used in Arabia in the days of the prophet, we learn that it was usually used to convey the idea of wise sayings of the older and

---

1 Tirmidhī : Ṣaḥīḥ, Tafsīral-Qur'ān, 5, 9-11 ; cf. Bukhārī : Ṣaḥīḥ, Tafsīru'l Qur'ān ; cf. A. b. Ḥanbal VI. 241.

more experienced members of the community. It was used in a sense equivalent to its early usage in Greece, that is, in the days of wise sages in pre-Socratic age. Like the change in its meaning among later Greeks, it began to indicate philosophy and medicine in the Islāmic world of later days. It was after the introduction of Greek philosophy among the Muslims that this change took place in its usage. We can safely conclude from this that the term as used in the Qur'ān was intended to convey a meaning similar to its usage among the Arabs in the days of the prophet, and in this sense it would primarily cover the Traditions of the prophet or Ḥadith, including both his actions as well as his sayings and in a wider sense it would include the sayings and actions of the other prophets and holy persons either reported by the prophet or by the previous holy books which were accepted as divine by the Muslims.

Another Qur'ānic verse is offered to support the theory of the two-fold mission of the prophet of Islām. The Qur'ān says, "He has made complete for you His favours outwardly and inwardly."[1] As this verse is addressed to the believers, it is said to indicate that the prophet was sent to complete both the blessings of Zāhir and Bāṭin, which the Sufis interpret as Sharī'āh and Ṭarīqah respectively. But according to the best annotators of the Qur'ān this verse does not split the teachings

1 The Qur'ān XXXI. 20.

of the prophet into two parts; rather it refers to the complete reformation that was brought about by his teachings. It refers to the worldly and political progress of the followers of the prophet, side by side with their spiritual and moral transformation. It blesses the followers of the prophet with a double reward here, and hereafter, on lines similar to those of the children of Israel. The Qur'ān says about them: "When Moses said to his people: O my people remember the favour of Allāh upon you, when He raised prophets among you and made you kings and gave you what He had not given to any other among the nations."[1]

In a similar way, the Qur'ān has laid down as a prophecy that among the Muslims also such persons shall be raised as shall be the spiritual guides and shining lights for the whole world and also that they shall be made the rulers, governors and kings of vast empires. So it actually happened as a natural result of the dynamic teachings of the prophet. His followers in his own lifetime became the spiritual guides for nations and not long after his death they succeeded in conquering Syria, Persia, Egypt and other parts of Africa, Asia and Europe. His companions were followed by able, learned and spiritual disciples who were in no way inferior to the prophets of Israel.

Some other interpreters take this verse to

1 The Qur'ān V. 20.

refer to the reformation of the private and public life of the faithful, brought about by the teachings of the prophet. They support their interpretation by quoting the Qur'ānic verse, which enjoins the Muslims to give up the indecencies both apparent and concealed. The Qur'ān says, "Say, My Lord has only prohibited indecencies : those of them that are apparent as well as those that are concealed."[1] In any case the interpretation offered by Sufis is far-fetched and cannot be supported by any tradition of the prophet.

Again, consider the Sufic interpretation of the Muqaṭṭa'āt In the beginning of certain chapters of the Qur'ān, there occur certain separate letters outwardly unconnected with the chapters and separate from one another if more than one. Some chapters begin only with one latter as Qāf and the others with more than one as Alif-Lām-Mīm. Sufis conclude from the use of these words in the Qur'ān that the prophet taught 'Ilmu'l-Bāṭin or Ṭarīqah (Path) as well as Sharī'ah or Law. The prophet never made an attempt to explain these letters, yet it is certain that they being a part of the Qur'ān could not be meaningless. No authentic saying of the prophet is known to exist about their explanation, and therefore the Sufis conclude that their meanings also have been taught by the prophet secretly, and that it is the function of the Shaikh to unfold their meanings. Consequently each

---

1 The Qur'ān VII, 33.

Shaikh tries to explain them according to his own light and understanding.

More than forty explanations have been offered as to their use and meaning. We shall refer to only a few most important ones. On the basis of positive historical evidence, however, some of the other explanations appear to be more credible than the mystic explanation of the Sufis.

In the early days of Islām when the literary superiority of the Qur'ān was considered to be the chief reason for its being God-sent, these separate letters were considered as an evidence of its literary grandeur. They were thought to have been placed in the beginning of the chapters to raise the literary standard of the Book and though appearing separate were considered to be intimately connected with the subject-matter of the chapter which they introduced.

Some annotators are of opinion that they indicate the gist and substance of the chapter before which they are placed. Just as Fātiḥah, the opening chapter of the Qur'ān, is a summary of the Holy Book,[1] in the same way these letters serve the purpose of expressing in a nutshell the contents of the chapters that follow them. This explanation has been objected to on the ground that if they are placed before chapters under some definite scheme, then why should they have been

---

1 Bukhārī : Ṣaḥīḥ, Tafsīru'l Qur'ān ; cf. Tirmidhī: Ṣaḥīḥ, Tafsīr ul-Qur'ān, t. 3, 4.

placed only before a few, and not before all? Why should only a few chapters have been thus summarised and not the rest?

In the second and third centuries of Hijra when Greek philosophy became the dominant passion of the Muslim men of letters, the theory of nominalism became more prominent, consequently a nominalistic explanation of these letters came into vogue. It was said that these isolated letters indicated the names of the chapters before which they were placed, as was evidently the case with the chapters Hā-Mīm and Qāf. But a name must be specific and proper. It does not serve the function of identification if it is applied to more than one thing. In the Qur'ān the same letters are used before more than one chapters, as for instance the letters Tā-Sīn-Mīm stand before the 26th chapter, as well as before the 28th.

The Sufis explain them by saying that they stand for various mystic names or attributes of Allāh. Some other writers believe that they stand for different things before different chapters and that no one principle of interpretation is applicable to all of them. Sometimes, they say, they indicate the names of Allāh, sometimes His attributes, sometimes they stand as brief signs for the articles of faith, and on other times they stand only for the names of the chapters which they precede. Take, for instance, the three letters Alif-Lām-Mīm, which stand before the second, the third, the twenty-ninth, the thirtieth, the thirty-first and the thirty-third chapters of the Qur'ān. Judge the explanation of these three letters as offered by the Sufis. Alif they say indicates Allāh according to the rules of brevity, and Lām indicates the Lawḥ or Tablet, on which the Qur'ān is believed to have been scribed before it was revealed unto the prophet, and Mīm, according to the same method, stands for Muḥammad. When therefore taken together they form a complete sentence meaning that Allāh has sent the Qur'ān unto Muḥammad. It appears to be a very apt beginning for those chapters which describe the Divine character and the heavenly source of the Book of which they form the parts.

There is no doubt that the explanation of certain verses of the Qur'ān as given by the Sufis is more satisfactory than the one given by the theologians. Specially those verses, which are mystic in nature, have been best explained by them. But in the Qur'ān, there are not many verses of this kind. Every verse can be given a mystical meaning, but sometimes it takes away the whole beauty of it and very often it does violence to the context. A good deal of service has been done by the Sufis in the direction of arranging, systematising and explaining the various names and attributes of Allāh that occur in the Qur'ān. This is the proper field of the Sufis and whenever they transgress this field they fare very ill.

Islām was an attempt to reform three different aspects of human activity: human beings as related, firstly, to their Divine Creator, secondly, to society, including family and other social institutions, and thirdly, to the rest of the world at large. The method that Islām adopted to reform humanity was to start with strengthening the bond of relationship between the created and the Creator, thus assuring a strong foundation for building up moral life. Sufism specially emphasised the first link in the process, and neglected the importance of relationship of an individual to society and the world at large.

So much intelligence of the Muslim Sūfis has been expended on the description of this relation between man and his Creator that it has become very difficult to throw it aside as mere rubbish. Let us take an instance. The problem of the soul or spirit is the foundation of all Sufi doctrines. It is with its progress and development, they say, that Sufism is chiefly concerned. The question about the essence of the soul was much in vogue in the days of the prophet as it is upto this day. When some one asked the prophet what the soul was, he was inspired to reply, "Say: Soul (Spirit) is by the commandment of my Lord and you are not given aught of knowledge but a little."[1] The problem of the soul was of philosophical nature

1 The Qur'ān XVII. 85; cf. Bukhārī: Kitābu'l 'Ilm.

and the object of the unbelievers in asking this question appears to have been to point out the prophet's ignorance of philosophical problems, although he had never claimed to be a philosopher or a learned scientist in the ordinary sense of these terms.

Indeed the creation of Adam, as described in the Qur'ān, supports the view expressed by this brief and novel answer about the nature and essence of the soul. According to the Qur'ān, the Creator made Adam from dust, breathed into him of His (own) spirit, and ordered the angels to fall down in obeisance to him.[1] Thus the creation of Adam was no less mysterious than the nature of the soul.

Such a brief answer offered a wide scope for speculation for the people of mystic tendencies. Consequently we find that voluminous literature was produced by mystic writers on this particular topic. The most interesting part of it is that which deals with the different stages of the development of the soul, in the course of its flight towards its original source, the Creator of all souls. We shall discuss this topic in detail in a later chapter.

It is important to point out at this stage that according to some annotators this brief and aphoristic reply to such a vast question is very signifi-

---

1 The Qur'ān XV. 29 and XXXVIII. 72.

cant, inasmuch as, it emphasises that we should not waste our time in discussing about things which are beyond our comprehension. They think that the attitude adopted by the Qur'ān in answering this question is a death-blow to mysticism and mystic tendencies. They consider this verse to be a serious warning to those who hope to find nothing in the Qur'ān except mystic doctrines. They support their statement by pointing out that the Qur'ān is silent not only about the nature of the soul, but also about the more philosophic problems like those of Substance, Essence of God, Matter and Energy of the Universe, etc., although it deals at great length with such Divine attributes as concern the relationship of human beings with their Creator.

The Sufis answer this objection by saying that this verse rather supports their claim to interpret the verses of the Qur'ān in a mystic sense. They point out, that the intention of the Author of the Holy Book in leaving such an important problem unexplained clearly indicates that its mystic exposition is perfectly justified. They believe that only a few verses of the Qur'ān are such as do not involve mystic doctrines. Therefore, they conclude that the Author of the Qur'ān Himself desires that a mystic explanation of such verses be given. This belief is responsible for a good deal of fiction, because often in the zeal of reading some esoteric meaning in the plain Qur'ānic verses Sufi writers make them look mysterious and unintelligible.

If we carefully think over this brief reference to the human soul in the Qur'ān, we find that this can be the only possible definition of the human soul. It is most in keeping with the spirit of the Qur'ān and Islām. According to the Qur'ān, God is the only Author and Creator of everything. But some of His creation He has made subservient to the interests of human beings. It says, "If you ask them who created the heavens and the earth and made the sun and the moon subservient, they will certainly say Allāh."[1] On another occasion it says, "Do you not see that Allāh has made what is in the heaven and what is in the earth subservient to you?"[2] Again, it lays down still more clearly, "And He has made subservient to you whatsoever is in the heavens and whatsoever is in the earth, all, from Himself."[3] As regards human beings He has created them subservient only to Himself. Man being the crown and cream of all His creations, all things have been subdued to his service, but man cannot be subdued to the service of any other creature except that of Allāh. Man is the master and purpose of creation but still a servant to the will of the Creator. His distinctive characteristic is that he is intended for the obedience and worship of his Creator. The spirit or soul being the active principle in man, and the essence of

1 The Qur'ān XXIX. 61; cf. also XXXI. 29.

2 *Ibid.* XXXI. 20. 3 *Ibid.* XLV. 13.

human nature, cannot be defined in the terms of any relation other than the one it bears to its Creator. To put it more logically, the differentia of man is this that he is created for the obedience of God only, and therefore, the active principle in him can be defined only in the light of this relationship.

This explanation is supported by the incident mentioned in connection with the creation of Adam. At the time of his creation God ordered the Angels who till then were the best of all creation to bow down in obeisance before him.[1] This proves that the human soul was created as superior to all other beings including the Angels. It is evident, therefore, that the definition of such a sublime thing in the terms of any relation other than that which it holds with its Creator would be to degrade its real position.

A sharp distinction has been made by the Qur'ān between the human soul and human consciousness. The Qur'ān does not deal with the question of the essence or origin of consciousness, but only with those aspects of it which are connected with morality and spirituality. This system of treatment has been consistently followed by the Qur'ān with respect to all such problems.

The Qur'ān refers to three kinds of consciousness, rather to three stages of its development in its progress towards its moral and spiritual ideal.

---

1 The Qur'ān II. 34; cf. *ibid.* XV. 29.

These three kinds are: an-Nafsu'l-Ammārah or Evil Consciousness, an-Nafsu'l-Lawwāmah or Balanced Consciousness, and an-Nafsu'l-Muṭma'innah or Satisfied Consciousness.

According to Islām, human nature is potentially good and it is on account of this potential goodness that it rises high towards its ideal, inspite of so many temptations and hindrances in the way of its progress. Muḥammad is reported to have said, "Every child is born a Muslim, his parents turn him to one faith or the other."[1] Compare this principle of human nature with its eternal sinfulness, a hypothesis introduced to prove and to make possible the redemption of sins by Christ. Once the principle of the potential goodness of human nature is conceded, the pernicious theory of redemption will contradict the mere rudimentary fundamentals of the ethical implications of a divine Revelation. It is for want of this belief in the inherent goodness of human consciousness, that Christianity has failed to satisfy the demands of moral human nature. Once you start with the inherent sinfulness of the human soul, the utmost that can be achieved is its redemption, but there will be no possibility of building a positive structure of morality, or a definite character.

Moreover, the theory of the potential goodness of human soul is a direct corollary of the infusion

---

1 Bukhārī: Ṣaḥīḥ, al-Janā'iz; Muslim: Ṣaḥīḥ Qadar; Tirmidhī: Ṣaḥīḥ, Qadar.

of the divine breath in the human structure. The best definition of the human soul, as I have already pointed out, is in the terms of its relation to its Creator, from which it follows directly that it must be potentially good.

According to the Qur'ān, the Sin of Adam, of which so much has been made by the Christians, was pardoned by Allāh when he wept and sincerely prayed for forgiveness after his expulsion from Heaven for yielding to the temptation of his enemy.[1] The Qur'ān mentions this sin only as an accident in the life of Adam, and not as an eternal curse affecting his whole life and even the life of all his descendants.

But it is to be remembered, that in the beginning the human soul is good only potentially. Like the acorn it is merely a possibility of developing into an oak if the soil and the surroundings are congenial. It has still to actualise its possibilities. If the strong winds of temptations blow, it can easily be swept away. It has very little of resisting power. It is at the mercy of natural forces and accidental circumstances, which happen to come in contact with it, and influence it. If Allāh helps it through this stage safely, then it is sure to become a great power. During its course of struggle against temptations and oppositions it often keeps asserting its natural inclination for goodness, by showing repentance and by pray-

1 The Qur'ān II. 39.

ing for forgiveness to its All Merciful Creator and Forgiver of sins. Even the most cherished creatures of God have to meet their own moral difficulties, so they also stand in need of forgiveness; therefore, it is meaningless that one creature should atone for the sins of others.

According to the Qur'ān even the consciousness of the prophets is not absolutely above the possibility of falling a prey to temptations. Human nature is morally the same to a great extent, both in the case of a saint and in the case of a criminal. Adam, as I have already mentioned, lent ear to the evil counsel of his rival and suffered the consequence, though he was completely pardoned afterwards. Similarly Joseph when invited to the evil deed by the Potipher's wife felt a little inclined to do her bidding, but the kindness of Allāh intervened and stopped him from committing the sin. Surely this is a great act of mercy to check a person from doing an evil thing which may result in his moral degradation. Joseph is himself reported by the Qur'ān to have said, "And I do not declare myself free, most surely (man's) consciousness is wont to command (him to do) evil, except such as my Lord has had mercy on."[1]

Allāh most surely intervenes in the case of those who believe in Him and who pray to Him for the same. He not only helps them in the

1 The Qur'ān XII. 52.

material advancement and spiritual progress, but also restrains them from committing sinful acts. Prophets are men and as such are liable to fall a prey to temptations, but God saves them from sins by arranging the chances in such a way that they desist from doing evil deeds. This favour of Allāh is not limited to prophets only, but every body who believes in God and prays to Him for this favour can receive it. Liability to fall a prey to temptations is simply an indication of the weakness of human nature and not of its inherent sinfulness, as the advocates of the theory of Redemption would have us believe.

The Qur'ān has accepted the theory of the sinlessness of the prophets as a class, not because they were above temptations, for they were human beings and as such possessed all the weaknesses akin to humanity, but because Allāh did not like that His Apostles should leave a record of evil deeds which might misguide their followers. Bad exemplars do not produce good followers; therefore, God-sent guides should set only good examples for the humanity. Even the sin of Adam, which has become proverbial and constitutes the foundation of the creed of a large section of humanity, was committed by him before he was sent as an apostle. According to the Qur'ān he was an apostle[1] but he was made apostle only when he was forgiven his sin for which he had to give up his

1 The Qur'ān III. 32; cf. *Ibid.* II. 37, 38.

pleasant abode in the gardens of Paradise. Therefore, the Qur'ān, unlike the Bible,[1] does not impute any evil deeds to any person, who is called the apostle of Allāh and who is sent to deliver His message to His human creatures.

The Qur'ān, therefore, clearly establishes the truth, that the prophets as a class are innocent and sinless, not because they are above the possibility of committing sins, for as human beings they are liable to all human temptations, but because Allāh saves them from sin in order to make their life an example and a guidance for others.

The next stage of the development of consciousness is called Balanced Consciousness. At this stage consciousness is introduced to the Law or the Message of Allāh. But it is only acquaintance so far. Its grasp of the Divine Law is not yet strong enough to ensure the complete abolition of evil from itself. Temptations do get the upper hand in controlling it now and then, but on the whole the good inclinations predominate the evil propensities.

The term used by the Qur'ān for this kind of consciousness is an-Nafsu'l-Lawwāmah, which means "the accusing self".[2] At this stage of consciousness one becomes self-introspective and critical

---

1 Old Testament: Genesis XIX. 31-38 concerning the prophet Lot; cf. *Ibid.*: I Kings XI. 1-10, wherein the prophet Solomon is blamed for an inclination towards Polytheism.

2 The Qur'ān LXXV. 2.

of one's intentions and deeds. The ethical criteria of differentiating between good and bad become developed to a perceptible degree. It is a stage of discrimination, of self-examination, at which the difference between right and wrong, between good and bad is clearly felt and perceived and the moral self becomes distinguished from the merely physical self of the first stage. The guidance at this stage also comes from Allāh but it comes rather through the internal principle of the law-abiding soul than in a miraculous way. It is at this stage that conscience merges out of consciousness. From mere awareness and perception it develops into a discriminating, comparing, rejecting and selecting consciousness.

When it obeys the divine Law continuously for a long time it attains its highest stage which the Qur'ān calls an-Nafsu'l-Mutma'innah or "Satisfied Consciousness". It is the highest stage of its spiritual development. It achieves this stage by constant and ceaseless struggle for doing good, and at the same time by firmly holding to a belief in the Source of all Goodness. Constant good actions and a consistently firm belief are the only means of arriving at this stage of the development of consciousness. Temptations will be present as they are inseparably bound up with human nature, but they will pass off without disturbing the serenity and calmness of such consciousness.

At this stage the mind will be quite full of peace and confidence in its Creator. It is with regard to such minds that the Qur'ān says, "Allāh is well pleased with them and they are well pleased with Him,"[1] and "O tranquil Soul! Return to thy Lord well pleased (with Him), well pleasing (Him)."[2]

Some characteristics of this stage of the development of consciousness are that it does not find fault with the working of its Lord. It does not question the advisability of the actions and the orders of its Creator. It is a condition of complete submission to its Master. It is further conditioned by the complete satisfaction of mind which is free from worries and cares of the lower animal instincts and impulses of human nature.

This stage is attained by complete obedience to the Law and the Will of God, by an undaunted faith in His Mercy, by a constant fear of His Omnipotence, by good actions done according to His express Law and with a view to seeking His pleasure and by avoiding all temptations, so far as possible. But without His guidance and kindness there is no possibility of attaining it, though at this stage His guidance works through faith and spirit. Thus there are three elements which are prominent at this stage. Firm faith in

---

1 The Qur'ān XCVIII. 8.

2 *Ibid*. XXLXIX. 27, 28.

God, good actions performed according to the Law, and His kindness. They are the three essential constituents which must be present in order that this stage of mental development may be achieved. This, in the main, is the Qur'ānic view of the three stages of the development of human consciousness. In the next chapter we shall discuss the mystic implications of this theory.

CHAPTER V.

EMERGENCE OF PRESENT SUFI DOCTRINES

It is after the age of early companions that Mysticism appears among the Muslims. It is a period in which a number of systems and orders cropped up in the Islāmic world. Each order was later divided into a number of branches, each branch representing a new off-shoot of the original views of the founders of different orders.

It was at this time that Muslims were busy in conquering the old empires and in laying the foundation of new ones. Learned Muslims were busy in creating encyclopædic systems in the domain of the different branches of learning. In short, this was the time when every member of the Muslim community, who had the least ability to lead, found himself at the head of a number of persons who were prepared even to lay down their lives at his command. The age of strict discipline had almost passed away. The principle of Khilāfat and centralization had been deprived of all its meaning except its form and name. Civil war had become the order of the day. There was bloodshed and devastation on every side. One sect against another, one province against another, and one general against another was vying for superiority and independence. The Fāṭimides had lost their secular power but were still respected and revered by many Muslims as descendants of the prophet.

It was the time when political unrest was at its highest in the whole Islāmic world. The conquered races could not find a better opportunity to destroy the basic strength of their rulers, who were chiefly Arabs. Persia took the lead. In spite of the fact that Persia had lost all its ancient institutions, the spirit of nationality was still there and it asserted itself at the time when the practical genius of the Arabs was being crushed by their own strifes.

The Muslims at large had become tired of constant struggle and ceaseless warfare. They longed for peace, and for a theory of religious life which might spare them from continual wars, which for the masses were becoming almost unbearable. Such a theory of life did not take long to come, and as soon as it was stated with appreciable clearness it had not to wait for followers.

The struggle was not only limited to the political domain of life, but the intellectual world of Islām was also full of controversies and dissensions. The rise of a class of Doctors of Law had converted the whole of the Holy Book into a system of legal doctrines. They considered the Qur'ān to be no more than a code to be acted upon and a code to judge only the legal aspect of the human relations. Some of them had interpreted the Qur'ān in a very superficial way. The reason for this superficial interpretation was not far to seek. Partly because Muslim rulers as the judicial heads of their governments required a ready-made code, and partly because by the vast expansion of Islām as a religion a large number of people had entered into its fold, whose mother-tongue was not Arabic, or who had not the literary capacity to interpret the Book for themselves, the learned Doctors had changed the Qur'ān and Sunnah into a formal code of dogmas and ceremonies. Each doctor, interpreting the Qur'ān according to his own principles and his intellectual capacity, differed from the rest, sometimes about very important points. So there came to exist among the Muslims as many schools of Law as there were doctors, each of whom was followed by a number of the faithful. In the beginning there was no hard and fast line of difference between the followers of these different schools, but later on great strictness began to be observed. Still later it was announced as a definite principle that a follower of one of the doctors must follow him in every detail, though in the beginning there was no such strictness and a Muslim could follow one doctor about one principle and another doctor about another principle. Nowadays this rigidity has become still more strict. It is accepted as a fundamental principle by the masses that a follower of Abū Ḥanīfah, for instance, must follow Abū Ḥanīfah or the doctors of Ḥanafī school, in all the details and interpretations of the Book and Islām. Unfortunately this goes by the name of consistency, although in reality it is nothing short of a gross inconsistency that contravenes the original intents and purposes of Islām. This kind of rigidity has helped not a little in banishing independent and free thinking out of the Muslim mind and has contributed a great deal to dividing the Islāmic world into so many watertight compartments of sectarianism, although sectarianism was so clearly condemned by the Qur'ān and by the prophet.[1]

All these doctors were more or less like jurisconsults of the early days of the Roman Empire. They were a class of persons who proposed to interpret the law of the Qur'ān. Their interpretation was free, rational and extensive and sometimes became an authority side by side with the Qur'ān, and not very rarely it superseded the letter of the law itself. Almost all such interpretations became an unalterable authority, sometimes during the life-time of their authors and usually after their death. Some of these doctors gave themselves a free latitude to interpret the Qur'ān, and consequently their interpretation was often superficial and unsatisfactory. Some critics have traced the cause of such interpretations in the

1 The Qur'ān VI. 160.

fact that some of these doctors held high official positions in the royal courts. In certain few cases this explanation may hold true, but in the majority of cases this view cannot be supported by historical facts. It was seldom that a founder of any one of these famous schools of law held a high official position in the court. The life of Abū Ḥanīfah (d. 150 A.H.), the founder of the Ḥanafī school is very instructive in this respect.[1] He is one of those illustrious leaders of Islām who suffered imprisonment, calumny, corporal punishment and death resulting therefrom, for not accepting the office of the chief judicial advisor to the ruling prince. Aḥmad b. Ḥanbal (d. 231 A.H.) is another instance of this kind. He was regularly persecuted by Al-Ma'mūn and his immediate successors al-Mu'tasim and al-Wāthiq for refusing to believe in the creation of the Qur'ān.[2] If he had yielded in this point, he might have been given a responsible position in the State. These doctors had the sense to understand that to accept such positions was to take a great risk in matters of conscience and faith. But unfortunately this rule was not strictly observed by their disciples. Even a learned person like Abū Yūsuf (d. 182 A.H.), who was one of those two distinguished disciples of Abū Ḥanīfah, who are unanimously accepted as of equal authority with their master by the followers of the Ḥanafī school,

---

1 Shiblī: Sīrat'un-Nu'mān, pp. 45, 48, 49 (Delhi 1915 A.D.)

2 Encyclopædia of Islam, Vol. I, p. 188.

could not avoid the temptation of accepting the office which was so contemptuously refused by Abū Ḥanifah.[1] It has been inferred from this that some of the followers of the original founders of these schools interpreted certain passages in the Qur'ān in such a way as to please their rulers.[2] But it is more likely that some of these interpretations were associated with the name of the original founders of these schools either by their ignorant followers or by their fault-finders and critics. The original founders of different schools were undoubtedly free from dishonesty and partiality. Their disinterestedness, impartiality, honesty of purpose, zeal for true interpretation and true representation of Islām, and their love for the founder of Islām have become proverbial. The result of this scholasticism and intellectual struggle, which was going on side by side with political strife, was evidently a search for a theory of life that might save the tired Muslims from physical, political and intellectual unrest. We have seen the Great War of Europe and have read about the European wars of Napoleon's days ; the result in each case was a desire for peace, for new theories of life that might end such struggles. It is only after such great wars that the necessity for a League of Nations is keenly felt.

But the grip of Islām on the mind of the masses

1 Macdonald : Muslim Theology, p. 96.

2 *Ibid.* p. 97.

newly converted, was still sufficiently strong. Therefore, this search for a new theory was essentially made in the direction of the reinterpretation of Islāmic doctrines. The life of the prophet and his companions was still fresh in the mind of the faithful. Those who have studied the Socratic movement in Greece can easily understand how the life of a great man can be interpreted in most contradictory ways. A simple man of Athens was taken as an ideal of ascetic life by Cynics on the one hand, and a mere pleasure-seeker by Cyrenaics on the other. Similarly much could be found in the life of the prophet and his companions to support the new theory of life and a new interpretation of the Qur'ān and Islām. The influence of the followers of other religions was in no way negligible in bringing about this change in ideas about life, but this influence helped to develop the worst aspect of this new theory.

The intelligent Muslims had begun to feel that constant wars were depriving them of the spiritual and ethical enjoyment of Islām. The wars also were degenerating into secular and factious feuds, and therefore, they were slowly losing their sanctity. The result of such wars was to make the masses devoted to worldly gains, exactly the thing which was prohibited according to the dictates of the prophet.[1] The life, therefore, in the Islāmic world was becoming superficial, shallow and completely

1 Bukhārī : Ṣaḥīḥ, Faḍ'u'l-Jihād.

devoid of all depth of morality and spiritualism. It was fast losing all its charm and seriousness. Superficial thinkers consider the life of that man to be the happiest who lives most heartlessly, having no regard either to his own rational self or to the suffering of others. Such men are far away from enjoying the real pleasures of life, which are the outcome of living in accordance with the highest principles of life. Pleasant life can be attained by him alone, who performs the duties of his life in the most conscientious way. Human pleasures as distinguished from animal pleasures are the only real pleasures for human beings and they can be attained by feeling most for others, and by controlling one's animal desires.

It was clearly realised by those who were trying to bring about a reformation, that a theory, not resting on the strong foundation of the idea of the unity of God, the central principle of the Islāmic faith, on the basis of which the prophet had worked his moral, spiritual and political reforms, could not be successful. This principle was again appealed to, as the cardinal truth for reforming the life of the faithful, who were tired of the constant civil wars. It was under the banner of the Unity of God that the faithful were bidden to rally again. But this time the doctrine was stated in a different way from that of the prophet's and was attended with certain weaknesses that were essentially connected with its new from. It was the abstract Unity of God that was taken up this time, a unity devoid of concrete relations with life.

How could this abstract Unity be connected with humanity, because by itself it could not be reduced into the terms of human relations ? Unless a connecting link could be found it would be useless as a theory of life, and unless it could reform human life it would fail to fulfil the primary object of its existence. The connecting link between the abstract Unity of God and human life was found in Love. But this human passion in having been declared as the connecting link was to a great extent deprived of its human aspect and sublimated into an abstract idea in order to befit the abstract Unity of the Divine Being. Again, this love must be all-enveloping and all-intoxicating, and must take precedence over all the other passions of the soul, if it is to guide the wandering human soul to the one Reality.

Psychologically it is impossible to limit the soul to the exercise of one passion alone. A soul that developed one passion only would not be called well developed and perfect. But it is possible to give preference to one passion over all the rest, and to make it the guiding principle of one's life and mould one's actions in its light. Sufis as the pioneers of this reformative theory considered it to be the best and most praiseworthy act to sit contemplating about the idea of God, and to be enraptured by His Love.

The only well-spent moment of our life, they would argue, was the one we devoted to His Contemplation and Love. Love being the divine element in human nature must be cultivated at any cost.

Some Sufis have tried to translate this abstract love into concrete relations of human soul with the Absolute. They have laid down three stages for the development of soul, each stage, becoming a starting point for the next. First stage, they say, consists in the service to humanity. At this stage you must prefer every human being to your own person. You must devote yourself to the service of His creatures. In the words of the prophet: "A (true) believer is he whom other people trust in regard to their person and property."[1] This statement was intended to stand for the definition of a true believer, but it was generalised by Sufis to define a good man. However, as stated by Sufis, it only defines a good man in the first stage of the spiritual advancement. It means that only that person deserves to be called good who can direct his words, thoughts and actions for the good of human beings at large. Sa'dī has said, "There is no prayer better than human service, and that it does not consist in counting the rosary, in prostrating on the carpet, or in wearing the gaberdine."[2]

---

1 Ṭaysīru'l Wuṣūl: Vol. I, p. 19.

2 عبادت بجز خدمتِ خلق نیست — به تسبیح و سجاده و دلق نیست

The second stage consists in keeping a watch over one's heart. It means that every person who desires to be one with God must purify his heart first. He must not allow his heart to be busy with evil thoughts. He must learn to avoid temptations and to overcome all mean passions. When one has guarded his heart against evil for a sufficiently long time, and God becomes sure of his sincerity, He engages his heart with Himself alone. Promotion to this third stage is only a free gift of God's kindness, though even the initial stage is impossible of attainment without His kindness. In the first two stages also the idea of God is the guiding and controlling principle. The service of humanity without the controlling idea of His Love is sure to entangle the seeker in a labyrinth of lower passions, and thus lead him to Hell and destruction. It is reported that Abū Yazīd Bisṭamī, the Shaikh of Shiblī, guided him through all these three stages of the development of soul, and after him many Sufis followed this practice. Even Ḥājī Wārith 'Alī Shāh, a well-known Sufi of India, observed the same practice in the case of his followers.

Other Sufis favour a different course which is almost the reverse of the one stated above. They say that one should first try to be one with God, think of Him alone and love Him. If one can do it the purpose of his life is fulfilled. If after you have surrendered yourself to Him, He likes that you should serve His creatures then He will appoint you for that purpose and only then will it be proper for you to perform this service. They say that if you begin such service without being ordered by Him, then there is the grave danger of your being caught in the snares of Satan, and instead of achieving anything you may miss the end in search of means. The leading Sufi who insisted upon this course was Shaikh 'Abdu'l Qādir of Jīlān, one of the most famous Muslim Sufis.[1]

A few standard writers on Sufism like Ghazālī, Mujaddid Aḥmad Sirhindī and Ibn Sīnā lay stress on different modes of mind through which the spirit of a Sufi must pass before it can attain the ultimate object of its search. They liken the progress of the soul to the travels of a seeker who before arriving at his destination has to pass through so many halting stations, each of which has first to be reached patiently in order that it might form the starting place for the next and ultimately for the last and the final stage.

They lay down that the first feelings of a seeker are those of bewilderment and surprise.[2] As soon as he crosses the boundary of the perceptible and the tangible, everything beyond it looks wonderful and surprising to him. Things to which he was so far accustomed being finite in

1 Ash-Shaikh 'Abdu'l Qādir Jīlānī: al-Fatḥu'r-Rabbānī, Sermon 26.

2 Mujaddid Aḥmad Sirhindī: Letters, Vol. III. Letter 33.

nature seem quite mean and negligible as compared with the things of the infinite world. When a seeker, therefore, first comes across the Infinite and the Limitless and compares his own limited nature and the nature of other finite things with it, he becomes astonished. It is further stated by Sufi writers that on account of the maddening influence of the feelings of wonder and surprise the seeker at this stage is likely to go beyond the limits of the Law and even of reason sometimes, particularly when the emotion of wonder is extremely strong and the power of controlling it meagre.[1] It is on the basis of this argument that a number of unreasonable and sensational sayings of certain Sufis are justified. The wild utterance of Manṣūr-al-Hallāj, "Ana'l-Haqq" (I am the Truth) hasbeen ascribed to the maddening influence of this emotion of wonder. European writers, particularly Dr. Nicholson, have credited Mansūr with laying the foundation of Mysticism among the Muslims.[2] This statement is quite justifiable if by Sufism we understand only Pantheism, a theory which was never accepted by the learned Muslim doctors nor even by Muslim Sufis of great repute, while attempts were made by many of them for setting up rival theories whose comparative claims as to their philosophic value

1 Mujaddid Aḥmad Sirhindī; Letters, Vol. I, Letter 43; cf. *ibid.* Vol. II. Letter 33.

2 Nicholson: Studies in Islāmic Mysticism, p. 79; cf. Mysticism in Islām.

we shall examine in detail in a later chapter. As I have already hinted, Islāmic Sufism started with the prophet himself and was followed by his companions to the letter. But in those days or even a little later, it was only a collective name for a set of practices, and had not developed in the form of dogmas and theories. Mansūr for the first time gave a practical impulse to Pantheism by announcing that he was the all-Truth, and by becoming a martyr to the cause of his announced principle. Thus doubtlessly he laid the foundation of a practice which could not succeed in catching the mind of the Muslims on an extensive scale on account of the vehement opposition with which it met from all quarters, but which nevertheless left its mark on the heretically disposed minds, specially because it was associated with the sacrifice of a human life—a fact which hardly ever fails to attract the attention of the ignorant and illiterate masses. It did not assume the form of a theory until a philosopher and dialectician of Muḥyu'ddin-ibnu'l-'Arabī's repute took it up and introduced it among the Sufis as the fundamental tenet of their beliefs and practices by bringing it in unison with the principle of Unity as preached by the founder of Islām.[1] He was followed by philosophers like Ibn Sīnā in whose hands it became an established principle of philosophy as well as of Sufism and

1 Nicholson : Studies in Islāmic Mysticism, p. 88 ; cf. Macdonald : Muslim Theology, pp. 261, 262.

thus worked as a mediator between the rival schools of philosophers and Sufis.

The second stage according to the Sufi writers is that of Self-negation. When the seeker has successfully crossed the wild field of wonder, and gets accustomed to the love of the Infinite, the passion of surprise slowly subsides into a feeling of self-negation. The feeling of one's insignificance as compared with the greatness of the Infinite slowly hardens into a feeling of the utter annihilation of one's self. Some Western writers on Sufism have pointed out that the self-annihilation of Sufism is equivalent to the Nirvana of Buddhism.[1] But it is a wrong interpretation of the theory of self-annihilation or self-negation, which is responsible for this misunderstanding. In reality there is a vast difference between the two.[2] In the case of Buddhistic Nirvāna it is pure and simple destruction of self-existence without any idea of aiming at a higher principle. Its object is merely to avoid life in all its forms because life according to the fundamental theory of Buddhism is evil and salvation is unattainable without a complete riddance.[3] It is self-negation without the hope of self-realisation or a higher self-regeneration. It is not difficult to see what an insignificant end it is and how far living beings can accept it as the good of their life and

1 Nicholson: Literary History of the Arabs, p. 391.

2 O'Leary: Arabic Thought, p. 191.

3 Prof. Flint: Antitheistic Theories, pp. 300-302.

the end of their actions. Nay even if the theory of Evolution had not been announced, even if the law of Inertia were not known to have been operating and even if the whole experience of the desire and struggle of the living beings to continue to live could be ignored, it would still not be difficult to pronounce without much consideration, that this kind of self-effacement would be absurd and purposeless. On the other hand a Sufi understands from the idea of self-negation an attainment of perpetual existence. He dies in body so that he may live for ever in spirit.[1] He dies in this world so that he may live for ever in the next. He dies from self so that he may live in God, the source of all life and all existence. He mortifies his flesh in order to live in the Eternal Spirit. Ḥāfiẓ of Shīrāz has said, "He whose heart is instinct with love, never dies; our eternal name is written for ever on the register of the world."[2] Such a state is the goal, the highest attainment of a Sufi. He lives a perpetual life, for he lives in Allāh, Who never dies. Some Sufis have interpreted this principle literally. From the phrase, "Living in Allāh," they understand something similar to a physical fusion of two things. It is this misunderstanding and misinterpretation which has invoked a good deal of criticism against this theory of union from the orthodox quarters.

---

1 Brown: Dervishes and Oriental Spiritualists, Chap. XVI.

2 "هرگز نمیرد آن که دلش زنده شد به عشق ثبت است بر جریده عالم دوام ما"

The final aim of a Sufi, according to this view, is the achievement of merger with his Beloved One. It is for the attainment of this final stage that he is prepared to give up everything including his own individuality. This is self-abnegation. For a Sufi self-abnegation is only a means of attaining the perpetual bliss and not an end in itself as the Buddhists conceive it.

Some Sufi writers point out that before a seeker can achieve the final merger of his self and his will into that of Allāh, he has to cross two other stages of merger, or to say more plainly there are three kinds of self-abnegation, the third of which is the last and final goal and consists in the abnegation of self into the self of the Infinite.[1] The first of these three, they point out, consists in the negation of one's self into the will of his spiritual guide. It means that as a preliminary step to the attainment of perpetual life into Allāh one has to annihilate his will in obedience to the precepts of his spiritual guide. The seeker has got to forget himself into the will of his Murshid.[2] The second abnegation is said to consist in the negation of one's will in obedience to the will of the prophet, who is unanimously taken for granted by all the spiritual guides as the highest and the

1 See 'Abdu'l Quddūs Gangohī: Letters; cf. also Ibnu'l 'Arabī: al-Futūḥātu'l-Makkīyah; and Farīdu'ddīn 'Aṭṭār: Mathnawī, Jawharu'dh-Dhāt, p. 473.

2 Farīdu'ddīn 'Aṭṭār: Mathnawī Jawharu'dh-Dhāt, Vol. II, p. 418 (Nawalkishore Press).

greatest of guides and the fountain-head of all spirituality and Taṣawwuf.[1] In this case the self which has realised itself into the will of his guide has got to be renounced for the sake of the obedience to the precepts of the prophet. Then comes the third stage of self-negation which, the Sufi writers say, consists in the abnegation of self in the obedience of Allāh. It consists in complete obedience to the commands of God, and at this stage all kinds of self are renounced for His obedience and His pleasure. It is this third stage of self-abnegation which is considered as the life of perpetual bliss and eternal happiness.[2] When the spiritual guide or Shaikh has guided his disciple unto the prophet and the prophet unto God, the object of search is fulfilled and after this for the seeker there is no death, no destruction.

But this view of the three-fold self-abnegation has not been accepted by a large number of Sufis, while it has been vehemently opposed by those who regard themselves as Muslims first and Sufis next, and who dislike to depart from the path of Islām. Great Sufis like al-Ghazāli, Shāh Waliu'l-lāh of Delhi and Aḥmad Mujaddid of Sirhind are some of those who are not in favour of this three-fold abnegation of self. Their account of the

---

1 Faridu'ddīn 'Attār: Mathnawī Jawharu'dh-Dhāt, Vol. II, pp. 419-420; cf. Jīlī's al-Insānu'l-Kāmil, tr. Dr. Nicholson in his "Studies in Islāmic Mysticism", pp. 105, 106.

2 *Ibid.* pp. 473-474.

spiritual stages has already been given.

There is no doubt that this theory is the outcome of degenerated Sufism. It came into vogue when the so-called spiritual leaders began to preach all sorts of doctrines to their ignorant followers, as the highest of Sufi truths. We find from historical evidence that so long as the hold of Islām was sufficiently strong over the mind of the public, the idea of the renunciation of self in favour of the spiritual guide did not appear as an active theory. The original founders of various Sufi orders did never clearly press for this belief as an essential doctrine of Sufi faith. No renunciation of self other than that one in favour of the prophet and God was known to them.

Another weakness of this theory lies in the fact that these three stages of renunciation do not come one after another. If they are to count at all, they must begin together. None is complete without the others. The first without the latter two is not only meaningless but heretical, the second without the third is useless, and the third without the second is not probably possible. The renunciation of self in favour of the prophet, unless for the sake of God, is meaningless and prohibited by the prophet himself. The prophet claimed to establish a Godly kingdom on earth and his personality without the central principle of his preachings, the notion of the Unity of God, is unintelligible. Should a Muslim disciple, when he is passing through the second stage, be neglectful of the idea of God? If so, then the second stage had better never come at all.

Again at the time when a disciple attains to the third and final stage, should he forget all about that self which was already renounced in the prophet? According to Islām the realisation of God is not possible without the help of the principles preached by the prophet. According to the Qur'ān, the commands of the prophet are so inseparable from those of God that to ask a Muslim to give up one for the sake of the other would do violence to his sentiments of faith.[1]

Next we examine certain qualities of the mind which some Sufi writers consider essential for the attainment of a perpetual bliss. Different qualities have been emphasised by different writers, but four of them are considered to be of great importance by almost all the writers. They are Patience, Ecstasy, Resignation and Obedience.

Patience as understood by the prophet and his early followers meant a capacity of resisting the evil. When the prophet was being persecuted by his people at Mecca, he bore it with a calmness of mind, which is rarely shown by ordinary persons under much less harder trials. He was tortured, insulted, abused and even threatened with a painful death, but he did not move an inch from what he considered to be the object of his life. This

1 The Qur'ān IV. 150.

quality of persistence in the cause of good, in face of all sorts of calamities, pains and threats has been called patience by the Sufis. It involves two elements, persistence in the cause of good or in the path of Allāh, as a Sufi would put it, and to face the tortures and resistance offered by Satan, or the opponents of truth with a cool mind without wincing or complaining. The followers of the prophet had to bear no less hardships in the propagation of truth and in the service of the faith. Therefore, Patience would mean resistance against all sorts of evil opposition, from whatever source it may proceed. It may proceed from the evil element in our own nature, from lower animal instincts of our own self, or from others, who may oppose us because we choose to stand for the cause of the good and the right.

The devil within us may be no less potent than the devil without us. Therefore, the quality of patience according to this interpretation would mean persistence in the path of Allāh in the teeth of all oppositions and hindrances. There is nothing in the Qur'ān or in Traditions which may restrict us from understanding the term in its general sense. But when the theory of the Abstract Love of God developed, Sufism began to emphasise the internal implications of the term rather than the external ones. It began to convey a quality of mind rather than a persistent activity.

The mental hindrance in the way of a firm belief were more emphasised than the actual opposition coming from the other evil-minded persons. To overcome the devil in us, to suppress doubts and lower passions, was conceived as the chief, if not the sole, characteristic of this virtue. It was in this way that the Greater Holy War (Jihād-i-Akbar) began to mean the struggle against our own evil nature and became a prominent theory among the Sufis. At this time the path was being slowly limited to Dhikr and contemplation, and the other obligatory commandments of Islām were being thrown into the background.[1] It represents the way in which the Sufis extended the meaning of certain technical terms of Islām and restricted others. The result of this distortion was not very agreeable on the whole.

When a disciple has passed through surprise and has escaped from the snares of Satan by patience and persistence, the will and knowledge of God are revealed to him through Ecstasy. Sufis believe that as Revelation or Waḥy is the means of revealing Divine knowledge to the prophets and Intellect to the philosophers, so is Ecstasy or Gnosis the means of His bestowing Divine knowledge on the Sufis, His chosen lovers.[2]

---

1 Dr. E. Lehmann: Mysticism in Heathendom and Christendom. Chap. on "Persian Mysticism".

2 Nicholson: Studies in Islāmic Mysticism, p. 9; cf. Nicholson: Literary History of the Arabs, p. 387. "The theory of Dhu'n-Nūn al-Miṣrī as presented in 'Aṭṭār's Tadhkiratu'l-Awliyā."

They say that it is a kind of inspiration which enables a created being, to become at one, and to converse with his Creator. When through extreme contemplation and great patience the mind of a seeker becomes enraptured and completely engrossed with Divine Love, God begins to bestow His knowledge upon him. It is an emotional state of mind in which feelings play an all important part and during which so many Sufis lose their consciousness and sometimes even their lives.[1]

According to some Sufis this state of mind can be attained through music. The Chishtī order of Sufis in India is the chief supporter of this view. But according to others music, which is prohibited by orthodox Islām, cannot be used for exciting the feelings of Divine Love. The Naqshbandī order of Sufis in India is the chief representative of this view. According to the Sufis of this belief, such feelings can best be excited by means of contemplation and Dhikr-i-khafī or by slowly muttering the name of Allāh. A third school of Sufis attempts at a compromise between the two extreme views, and says that only such music is prohibited as helps to promote lewdness, or stirs up the lower animal passions in us. Reciting the Qur'ān in a musical tone, or singing the praises of God or His

---

1 Jāmī: Nafaḥātu'l-Uns (Calcutta, 1858 A.D.), p. 698. (In connection with the life of 'Aṭṭār, Jāmī gives the account of a dervish who thus lost his life.)

prophet is not prohibited by Islām. They believe that music in itself is neither prohibited nor allowed by Islām. If its object is to rouse in us the love of God or that of His prophet then it is laudable, but if it is intended to stir up in us the lower and mean passions, then it is sinful and condemnable. The order of Qādiriyyah in India represents this view.[1]

In my humble opinion the stimulus for Ecstasy must come from the spirit alone, since God, Whose love causes and demands this state of mind, is purely a Spiritual Being. An excitement coming through senses can at most find its outlet through senses and would ordinarily leave the depths of soul untouched. It is through contemplation and meditation alone that this faculty of soul can best be developed. Mental excitement attained through music is a feeble imitation of the real Ecstasy that stirs the very depths of the soul.

Nothing like Ecstasy was known to the prophet and his companions. A complete absorption in the contemplation of God, during the time of their prayers, was a common thing to them. There is hardly any difference in the mental absorption of the prophet and his companions and the ecstasy of the later Sufis, except that in the case of the former this absorption was ordinarily during the time of the

1 Mujaddid Aḥmad Sirhindī: Letters 266, 285; cf. Ḥasan Sanjarī: Fu'ādu'l-Fu'ād. Ḥasan Sanjarī was one of the disciples of Niẓāmud-dīn of Delhi.

canonical prayers and was not brought about artificially by force of music or otherwise and was not regarded as a means of the transmittance of the knowledge and will of God. The only means of knowing the will of God to them was through the revelation of God to His prophet and through the sayings and actions of the prophet himself. This illustrates the process how the Sufis gradually developed the idea of direct revelation, the only source of which in the early days of Islām was the divine message to the prophet.

Ecstasy naturally leads to Resignation to the will of God. The seeker must resign his will to that of God if he is really to learn anything of His will and knowledge through Ecstasy. Complete resignation of one's actions, one's will and even of one's self to the will of Allāh, was one of the cardinal principles of the teachings of Islām and it was duly appropriated by the Sufis, only with a little exaggeration. According to the original theory of Islām, a human being never lost his individuality and his independence, while according to later Sufis the highest development of self was identical with the merging of self in some other self. About resignation the Qur'ān had taught the prayer, "I[1] entrust my affairs to Allāh.

The theory of resignation implies that everything that has been given to us including

1 The Qur'ān XL. 44.

our life is only a gift from Allāh, while all these things really belong to Him. Since, therefore, He is the real owner of all these things, including our lives, we have no claim or right to their ownership as such.[1] If He grants anything it is His kindness, bounty and grace, but if He takes away anything from us, we have no right to grudge, or complain, because we were not its owners. We are simply the users and trustees of His things. In this connection Traditionists relate an occurrence about Umm Sulaym, the wife of Abū Talḥah, a well-known companion of the prophet. It illustrates the attitude of resignation that was adopted by the early followers of the prophet. Abū Talḥah had gone out of his house for work. His child died in his absence. His wife did not show any sign of sorrow or lamentation, and made the child lie down on a cot as if it was asleep. When her husband came back she did not tell a word about the occurrence. After he had finished his meals and taken a little rest, his wife asked his opinion about a trust saying, "Some one had entrusted a thing to us, today he asked back his thing, what should I have done?" "You should have returned his thing to him without the least hesitation" was the rejoinder. "That have I done," continued she. "Here is your child. God had bestowed it on us and had made us its

---

1 Ibn Qayyim al-Jawzī: Ṭarīqu'l Hijratayn, Vol. I, Chap. I. Ḥaqīqatu'l-Faqr.

guardians, but today He called it back to Him, and I accepted His call cheerfully, since the thing called for was his. Similarly must you feel about the whole occurrence." Without sorrow or tear they buried the child next morning.[1] This is a remarkable expression of the feeling of resignation and this attitude the Sufis want each disciple or seeker to take whenever anything happens according to the will of Allāh. Some people may call it a submission to the unavoidable. No doubt, resignation does involve the feeling of submission to the inevitable, but it gives a flavour, a particular colour to the feeling of submission. Resignation may be submission, but it is not submission to the dead, mute and heartless forces of nature, but submission to the will of a Living, Acting, Intelligent and Responsive Personality, Who can alter the inevitable without giving reasons for it, and Who can change the course of forces and laws of nature if He so wills. So resignation indicates an active attitude of mind, while submission only implies a passive attitude. A person submits simply because he believes that it could not be otherwise, and the circumstances could not take any turn other than that which they took. Resignation is submission to a higher will, while submission is only a passive acceptance of the inevitable. Similar must have been the consideration of Abraham when he was

1 Bukhārī: Ṣaḥīḥ, Janā'iz; cf. Abū Dā'ud : Sunan, Janā'iz ; cf. Tirmidhī: Ṣaḥīḥ, Janā'iz.

taking his only son with him for sacrifice, according to the order of his Creator. He must have calculated and mused within himself, "I and my wife, were too old to get a child in the natural course of affairs. Allāh gave this son to us out of His kindness, and grace; now that He wants me to send this boy back to Him, let him go. I was simply his guardian. May my sins be pardoned to boot!" How much of pain and worry we could be saved from, if we but adopted this attitude of mind towards all happenings!

It is to develop such feelings of resignation that Islām has brought in fatalism, which has been so much criticised by its opponents and so much misused by the Mullās. The Qur'ān says, "No evil falls on the earth or on your own souls, but is in a book before We bring it into existence. So that you may not grieve for what has escaped you, nor be exultant at what He has given you."[1] Strict fatalism devoid of all feelings of resignation implies that when a thing has happened or must happen and its course cannot be altered, it is simply useless to cry over it; while resignation over and above this implies that whatever God does is for the best, and therefore we should not desire its occurrence in a different way, because that would be a desire for the worst world. We should consciously and actively subscribe to the Will of God.

---

1 The Qur'ān XVII. 22, 23.

On this principle we should have no desire, since our desires when fulfilled might not bring very happy results for us. Thus a Sufi suspends all his desires and waits for the will of God. Islām had taken a different view about this position. It had encouraged begging things from the Creator, and to that effect certain prayers were mentioned in the Qur'ān which were uttered by different prophets. The idea of asking necessities from God indicates one's faith and complete reliance on Him, and complete resignation to His will. If a man totally relies upon God for everything, however small, then he will never grudge or grumble if God does a thing as He likes. Accordingly the prophet is reported to have said, "Everybody is granted his prayer by Allāh, provided the creature does not desire its early fulfilment, and does not say that he had prayed for such and such thing and it was not granted."[1]

The difference between the view of a Sufi and that of early followers of the prophet about resignation is that a Sufi would suspend all his desires and would not beg the fulfilment of any of them from his Beloved One, while the latter humbly submitted their desires great or small to His will. If He thinks his desires fit, they would be granted, and if they are not granted there would be no complaint. The attitude that a true Muslim would take on such an occasion would

1 Bukhārī: Ṣaḥīḥ, Kitābu'd-Da'wāt.

be, that perhaps the fulfilment of such and such desire should have been harmful for him, therefore, by its non-fulfilment God averted that calamity from befalling him. Thus the prophet is reported to have prayed: "O God if the thing I desire is according to Thy will then make it a blessing for me, but if it is against Thy will, then turn this thing out of my heart and my heart from it."[1] Thus resignation of one's will to that of God, according to the Islāmic conception, means humbly submitting one's desires to His kind sanction or rejection without the least grudge or complaint.

Suspension of desires by later Sufis was, to some extent, justified by their mode of living. They had renounced the world, so their desires were reduced to the minimum. The few they had were being fulfilled by the rich Muslims, unasked for, without any effort on their part. Thus they had few things to pray for. But to limit the desires was also to limit the occasions of praying to God for their fulfilment. In this way the Sufis substituted an intellectual contemplation of God for an active reliance on Him.

In this manner the more Sufism was becoming limited to monasteries, the more it was losing the simplicity of Islām. The more the Sufis renounced the world, the farther they went from the facts and realities of life and became a class of

1 Mishkāt; Istikhārah.

theorisers without hard and substantial facts of real life to support their theories. The influence of other religions on Islām has always been to take away its simplicity, its charm and its representation of real life. Islām was the only religion that gave a real and comprehensive interpretation of life and used all the facts of life to support its doctrines of reality and moral reformation. It never allowed its followers to get out of touch with realities of life even for a moment. The founder of Islām was afraid of foreign institutions in this respect and had therefore warned his followers in clear words by saying, "There is no monasticism in Islām."[1] But the Sufis, carried by the flood of reaction against the secular struggle, became supporters of the opposite and pernicious elements of the neighbouring faiths.

The next question arises how we can learn to resign our will to the will of the Almighty. A Sufi would say that the best way is through obedience. When you begin to obey Him He will show you the right path. The early followers of Islām agreed upon the principle that the obedience required was of God and of His prophet. The Qur'ān had laid down, "Obey God, and obey the prophet, and obey those amongst you who hold the command."[2] It was often repeated in the Qur'ān that every prophet in every age asked the faithful

---

1 Aḥmad b. Ḥanbal: Musnad, Vol. VI, p. 226 (Cairo 1330).

2 The Qur'ān IV. 59.

to obey God and himself.[1] But the later Sufis added the obedience to the precepts of the Shaikh as a third duty, and emphasised that the obedience should be complete, unquestionable and blind. Now the question is whether this obedience is quite consistent with the commandments of Islām ?

We may say that in the case of a spiritual guide it must be reasonable, but in the case of God and His prophet it must be complete, and unconditional, since, in this case, the command comes from an authority, which *ex hypothesi* is the source of all reason and wisdom. In such a case it is unreasonable to ask reasons for every command which is to be obeyed. It does not mean that reason is to be condemned and to be altogether eliminated from human nature in religious matters. It only means that this faculty must first be educated and trained in the light of the absolute faith in God, the source of all reason, and then it might be in a position to pass judgment on His commands. Crude reason, not well versed in the science of His Love, might make blunders in understanding His doings, just as a layman not well up in the principles of physics might never give a true explanation of a simple physical phenomenon. It is unfair, therefore, and unnecessary on the part of those, who are not well versed in the principles of theology and Sufism to pass judgment on the principles of these sciences, simply on the basis of an untrained and uneduca-

1 The Qur'ān IV. 64.

ted general reason. Reason, therefore, unless well trained in the love of God is not a good judge of the actions and commands of God. Hence obedience to the commands of Allāh should be unqualified and complete, while obedience to the prophet qualified only by the command of God.

Thus obedience, followed by resignation with ecstasy and patience, guides the traveller to the path of God, to perpetual life, and to an everlasting existence in Him. These are the four essential qualities of mind that keep up a disciple persistent in his efforts of seeking his goal.

We may briefly summarise the characteristics of this age by saying that it was an age of founding new kingdoms, new schools of philosophy, of theology, and of jurisprudence, and Sufism was not lagging behind the general onward movement of Islāmic thought. Relying upon the asceticism and austerity of the life of the prophet and his companions, the Muslim intelligentsia was busy in finding out new doctrines as a cure for the Muslim mentality that was inclining towards secularism, and of these doctrines that of Sufism was one and the foremost. The founders of different Sufi orders came from different people and different countries. Each of them gave a version of life suited to the spiritual needs and mental habits of belief of his own people. But all of them agreed in taking life seriously, in turning away from frivolities and struggle for minor goods, towards a deeper significance, which as Islām had decided could be attained only through the deep love of and obedience to God, the source of all good.

The founders of Sufi orders, or at least most of them, were very good Muslims, and followers of the prophet, and indeed they had accepted Sufism with a pious wish of reforming the Islāmic world. They hated the world and worldly things but they did not believe in its renunciation, for they clearly realised, that after renouncing it there remained no hope of reforming it. At first this renunciation took the form of avoiding the company of kings and courtiers, but under the influence of monastic religions like Buddhism and Christianity it slowly developed into seclusion and loneliness.

The various founders of Sufi orders earned their livelihood with their own hands, as Islām had taught them to do, but slowly there arose a class among their followers who began to live upon their profession of Sufism, and not a few among them began to live upon actual begging, which was completely forbidden by the prophet.[1]

The early founders of various orders had probably calculated Sufism as a means for the propagation of Islām.[2] This idea is not clearly expressed anywhere in the writings of any Sufi, excepting the books of a few theologian Sufis, like al-Ghazālī, but it can be inferred from their actions and their ways

1 Bukhārī: Ṣaḥīḥ, Wujūbu'z-zakāt.

2 Prof. Margoliouth: Mohammadanism, pp. 211-12.

of living. Most of the founders of different orders are said to have converted the non-Muslims to Islām by thousands. Shāh Niẓāmu'd-dīn of Delhi, Shāh Mu'īnu'ddīn Chishtī of Ajmer in India, Shāh 'Abdu'l-Qādir of Baghdad and various others are associated with the movement of conversion to Islām. Out of the later Sufis very few appear to have given any thought to this practical aspect of the doctrine of Islāmic Sufism.

These early founders never made an attempt at distorting the meanings of any verse of the Qur'ān or of any saying of the prophet. They acted according to the Book and the Traditions in a very orthodox manner.[1] They based their doctrines on the Qur'ān and Sunnah, and they are reported to have been highly pious. They did not dissociate themselves from the Muslims. They lived and died among them, and were honoured and revered for their strict unitarian views, their extreme piety and love of God, their pious actions and good manners and their public service.[2] Only they waged war against the unreflective life, trivial desires, irreligious actions, impious motives and most of all against the frivolous interpretations of the Kitāb and Sunnah that were becoming the fashion of the day in the hands of the theologians and lawyers. They hated superficial life, outward cere-

---

1 See the account of Abū Yazīd Bisṭāmī by Ibn Khallikān tr. by De Slane, p. 662.

2 Prof. Margoliouth: Mohammadanism, p. 112.

monies, mere habitual performance of religious obligations, and strict observance of certain formalities which the learned doctors of Islāmic law had sometimes over-emphasised. What a sacrifice of the kernel for the shell! That is a great loss the Sufis would say. It is the heart which is cared for by Allāh and not mere formal actions or habitual performance of prayers and fasts. Rūmī says: "Verily, God does not see the outward form or the spoken word. He judges only by the inner heart and the mode of living."[1] It was this protest against the current mode of living and interpreting the two chief Islāmic authorities of the Qur'ān and Traditions that gave an attraction and force to the movement.[2] Its essence was the idea of the Unity of God, appreciable through pure and abstract love, and it gained its force because of the frivolous mode of life lived by the Muslims at the time.

Miracles.

A number of strange stories and uncommon miraculous occurrences have been associated with the early Sufis by their biographers, specially when the biographer happened to belong to their order.[3] But most of these records are unauthentic and unreliable when judged by the historical criteria. Most of these biographies were written in the third or

---

1 ما برون را ننگریم و قال را ما درون را بنگریم و حال را

2 Nicholson: Literary History of the Arabs, pp. 384-85.

3 Siyaru'l-Aqṭāb and Nithār 'Alī's life of Ḥallāj; cf. Prof. Margoliouth: Mohammadanism, p. 200.

fourth generation after the great Sufis had passed away and no critical acumen was exercised in collecting the material about them. Their contemporaries hardly mention anything about such miracles although they speak highly of their piety and their moral and religious fervour. We should also remember that most of such biographies were written when saint-worship had taken deep root among the Muslims, and when they looked upon the Shaikh as a divine being.

The compilation of treatises and doctrines of Sufism began in an age, when a true perspective of Islām was lost. We possess a fairly large number of treatises, letters, sermons and poetic collections of the founders of some of these orders. Nowhere in any one of these works have they referred to such miraculous performances. Some later writers have no doubt on occasions mentioned such miracles worked by the early founders, but it was simply with a view to giving them a halo of sanctity after the fashion of Christian and Hindu mystics.

We also find from the sermons and other works of those early Sufis that they attached very little importance to the possession of the power of performing miracles. Study the sermons of Shaikh 'Abdu'l-Qādir, who is popularly called the guide of guides, the famous founder of the Qādiriyyah order, or any other Sufi among the early founders, and you will find that they never based their arguments or their appeals for reformation on any miraculous powers possessed by themselves or by others.[1] Abū Yazīd al-Bisṭāmi used to say, "When you see a man possessing miraculous powers so as even to mount in air, let not that deceive you, but see if he observes God's commands and prohibitions, if he keeps within the bounds imposed by religion, and if he performs the duties which it prescribes."[2] This represents the attitude of the early Sufis towards miracles. They were true followers of Islām and as such they were aware of the truth that reformation could only be successful if it were based on the bed-rock of the Unity of God, and His fear and love. It is also to be noted that they had not discarded the fear of God as a motive for spiritual and moral actions, as it was done by later Sufis.[3] They emphasised the same eternal truth that was taught by the prophet of Islām that there was only one God and He alone deserved to be feared or loved.

Some great Sufis even among the later authorities have positively refused to consider miracles as the test of spiritual excellence. Out of a legion of names those of Imām Ghazālī, Mujaddid

---

1 *e.g.*, in his al-Fathu'r-Rabbānī; cf. Nicholson: Studies in Islāmic Mysticism, pp. 66, 67. The attitude of Abū Sa'īd towards miracles, one of the few passages that are based upon the statement of the saint himself, is uncompromising; cf. Mujaddid Aḥmad Sirhindī: Letters, Vol. II. Letter 92.

2 Ibn Khallikān, Vol. I: account of Abū Yazīd Bisṭāmī, tr. by de Slane, Paris, p. 662.

3 O'Leary: Arabic Thought, p. 184.

Aḥmad Sirhindī, and Shāh Isma'īl of Delhi may be mentioned as representatives.[1] This view is a reaction against the frivolous and childish tendencies that have been lately developing among the Sufis.

It is rather unfortunate that the writers on Sufism, specially Western, like Professor Nicholson, Professor Margoliouth and others, have attached such a great importance to documents of dubious authority.[2] They have relied chiefly on such

1 Mujaddid Aḥmad Sirhindī: Letters, Vol. II. Letter 92; cf. al-Ghazālī al-Munqidhu mina'ḍ-ḍalal, Statement 7 (Ḥaqīqatu'n-Nubuwwat); cf. Isma'īl Ṣirat-i-Mustaqīm and Taqwiyatu'l-Imān.

2 (a) See Nicholson's Literary History of the Arabs, p. 145, how against the claim of the celebrated Ibn-Qutaybah, that no other religion has such attestations, he, simply on the authority of Nöldeke, records the opinion of another Muhammadan to the contrary, without even giving the name of the man. Again, see the same book (p. 403) where the author refers to the report of Ṣadru'd-dīn, a disciple of Ibnu'l-'Arabī, how his Shaikh met the souls of previous saints and prophets.

(b) Again, see p. 88 of the Studies in Islāmic Mysticism by the same author, where he quotes a saying of the prophet, "Whosoever has seen me, has seen Allāh," which was never uttered by the prophet even according to the traditionists of very doubtful authority. The author perhaps means to refer to a true tradition of Bukhārī and other authentic traditionists, "He who saw me in the dream saw me truly, for Satan cannot assume my form." (Bukhārī: Ṣaḥīḥ, Kitābu't T'abīr).

Again, on p. 106 of the same book he reports another saying of the prophet, "God created Adam in His own image." It may be a quotation from the Bible but the prophet never said such a thing which contradicted his religion so profoundly, as he always preached against image worship of any kind.

(c) Prof. Margoliouth: Mohammadanism, p. 196, where he refers to the common fallacy of expressing in the form of tradition any idea believed to be good. This is an awful distortion and misunderstanding of the nature and value of traditions.

records as hardly possess any historical value. It is true that very few biographies of these early saints are available, particularly the accounts left by their contemporaries; therefore a student in order to say something about them, has perforce to rely upon these documents. But keen insight and thorough training are necessary in order to thrash out rare pieces of truth hidden under the heap of exaggeration and falsehood. If a Sufi has himself written anything then much about him can be gathered from his writings and if that is not the case, due allowance must be made for the relationship of the writer with the saint, for the reasons that led him to write the account, and chiefly the learning, the historical sense and the training of the writer. It can safely be said, therefore, that if the biographies of these saints are tested on some such reasonably severe criteria, more than half of them will be found to consist of nothing but rubbish, exaggeration and mythology. It is the only part of Islāmic literature which is mythological, and there is no doubt that this way of writing about their saints was borrowed by Muslim biographers from Christians, Iranians, Jews and Indians. Take any book from Indian, Persian or Christian literature of pre-Islāmic days, which gives an account of a saint, it would be quite apparent that the tendency of the writer is towards mythology, and towards deifying the saint. The Qur'ān had said with reference to Christians and Jews, "They have taken their doctors of law and their saints for Lords beside Allāh."[1] The miracles which were associated with the names of these saints were more or less considered the grounds for their deification,

It is on this account that the books on mysticism written by Western scholars do not give an accurate account of the authors of mysticism and their doctrines. They have chiefly relied upon the records which were written long after the death of saints, by their devoted followers or descendants, after the fashion of Christian and Indian biographers.[2] It appears that they have not taken pains enough to go through the works of saints themselves, if there existed any.

Still it cannot be categorically denied, that miracles were sometimes performed by the saints or that miracles are possible. Many of these saints are reported to have known many branches of occult sciences. Telepathy, heart-reading, suggestion and spiritual healing are known to have been abundantly practised by many of them. Many instances of their miraculous performances have reached us through writers whose authority we have no reason to doubt.[3]

1 The Qur'ān XI. 31.

2 In this connection see Prof. Nicholson's statement about Abū Sa'īd from Muḥammad b. Munawwar who was a descendant of Abū Sa'īd. The book which he relies upon is by some unknown descendant.

3 Jāmī: Nafaḥātu'l-Uns (Cal. 1858 A.D.), pp. 23-31.

There is nothing strange about any one of these practices. Almost every human being with a little development of the power of concentration and meditation can perform these feats and probably more, only that the firm believers in one God, since they can concentrate their attention on Him whenever they like, can learn their performance with greater ease and quickness. Some people have contended that a miracle worked through the agency of developed human powers will be different in nature from one granted by God. In fact each miraculous occurrence is different according to the source from which it proceeds, just as two apparently similar effects differ in their essence according to the real nature of the causes from which they proceed, or just like the two seemingly similar actions of a man that differ according to the difference in the nature of motives from which they spring.

This whole discussion may be ended by laying down a principle which I have inferred from the general perusal of Sufi literature and which will be drawn by every one who reads their works carefully, that the miracles were not considered an essential element of Sufism by the early saints. They do not base their arguments on miracles, nor do they refer to them very often. Some have actually condemned them as being no test of spiritual progress, and others have limited them to the prophets alone, and almost all have considered them to be the voluntary gift of God's grace, without claiming to possess any power in themselves for their performance. In this they have only followed the prophet, who, whenever asked to show a miracle, always replied that they were dependant upon the will of God alone.[1] The Qur'ān had unequivocally stated that any number of miracles would not change the faith of the doubters. No amount of miracles can convert people to the truth. The prophet was always anxious to avoid the implication that the miracles could be the test of truthfulness or of the spiritual eminence of any person. The Books believed to have been sent by God prior to Islām had appealed to people for their acceptance as true on the ground of the miraculous statements which they purported to make about the founder of the faith. Even after Muḥammad many persons who falsely claimed to be prophets but who in the long run were not recognised as such, had tried to rest their claim on miracles, sometimes very trifling and childish. It is very natural that a person who claims to be heaven-sent should support his claim by some unusual occurrences. But the prophet of Islām positively avoided to take advantage of any such occurrence even if it happened to take place in the natural course of things.

In the life of every human being there occur many things in the world that cannot be fitted

1 The Qur'ān VI. 110 and XVII. 93.

in the already ascertained principles of nature. It is one of those truths that have often been invoked by scientists to support the theory of the infinitude of reality and knowledge. Every day there happen as many things under our very eyes that cannot be explained on the grounds of Natural Laws already ascertained. Even from the scientific point of view such occurrences are miracles, for they are not explicable at the time of their occurrence. After such a phenomenon has passed away we modify our previous theories or invent new ones to explain it, to appropriate it, to understand it, and to assimilate it to our already existing system of knowledge. Ordinary human beings are usually so busy in earning their daily bread, in merely living out their life, that they hardly take notice of such occurrences, and if they ever happen to be thrust upon their attention they soon forget them. Either the scientists take notice of them in order to make them their own, or those who have a very keen power of observation record them for the sake of public utility. The prophets belong to the second category; therefore in proportion to the keenness of their power of observation they take notice of such phenomena and draw inferences from them. It is only impostors who always search for occurrences of extraordinary nature to support their claims, stating that such extraordinary things have been made to occur by heaven to support their cause or that they have been performed by themselves on account of their possession of extraordinary powers.

The prophet of Islām, for the first time in the history of the world, boldly announced the principle that miracles were no test of one's truthfulness or of one's being heaven-sent. He fearlessly proclaimed that the Qur'ān, his own moral life, his promulgation of the law of God, according to which He helped the faithful and punished the unbelievers, were the only tests of his truthfulness as a messenger of God. His only son Ibrāhīm is breathing his last, and just at the time of his expiry the sun is eclipsed. Credulous persons are heard saying that even the heavenly bodies are lamenting the loss of his son. He is conscious that his mere silence at hearing this assertion would mean his consent to it and would likely convert a large number of the credulous people to Islām, his most cherished desire throughout his life. But truth cannot thus be trifled with. It cannot be sacrificed even for million lives not to speak of a few conversions. He is probably also aware that a conversion on such a flimsy ground would not be very reliable and may be short-lived. He addressed the people saying, "The sun and the moon do not get eclipsed in consequence of the death or birth of any body."[1] In this way he once for all closed the way for conversion to a particu-

1 Bukhārī: Ṣaḥīḥ, Bābu'-Kusūf.

lar faith by means of miracles. He was well aware which faculties of the soul must be appealed to in order to win a person to the noble cause of truth, of love and worship of God. He knew well that a faith based upon flimsy grounds of miracles, upon the credulous aspect of human nature, would be just like a plant rooted in sand. Whenever there will be a shower of rain, whenever the right understanding of things will come, the whole belief will go overboard with its sandy foundation. With the development of reason and intellect such a belief is sure to be neglected, trampled upon and forgotten.[1]

Coming back to our original theme of miracles,

---

1 An illustration, if one is needed, for such a clear fact may not be far to seek. One of the chief elements of the faith of Christianity being the miraculous deeds of Christ, on account of which his miraculous personality was deified, the whole faith became weak and powerless with the development of intellect and reason. It is quite possible that its grasp might again revive among the Africans who on account of their gross ignorance are still credulous, but there is little hope of its revival and getting a firm footing, wherever it clashes with Islām which is equally suited for the learned and the ignorant, on account of its simple tenets But when Islām comes in contact with civilisation different from its own, the result is quite different. To a developed intellect it does not offer miracles for its being acceptable, but offers a theory of life, moral transformation and a code of good laws all based upon reason and common sense. It presents the fewest possible dogmas and ceremonies to be observed. It presents a law that leaves almost complete independence to the individual in the choice of his moral actions, only binding him by means of general principles. This attribute makes it highly adaptable to every land, every race, every nation, every society and every stage of civilization.

we can safely lay down that the early founders of Sufism followed the prophet in not attaching any importance to miracles as an argument for their superiority of will or for proving any theory of their own.

Gradually Sufism developed into a system. The early Sufis had no doubt laid down certain theories, certain modes of interpreting the Qur'ān and life, but in their ordinary life they followed the common obligations and precepts of Islām. They performed Dhikr in a simple way like ordinary Muslims as the Qur'ān had enjoined upon them.

In short, the path followed by the early Sufis was the path of the prophet and his companions in almost all important questions of theory and practice. Only in a few cases they showed a tendency to depart from the original simple path of Islām, and it was not difficult to detect in which direction the wind was blowing and what the result of all this deviation would be. The most important change that was coming over the Muslim society was that the Muslim public was being divided into classes, sects, schools and orders, and each group was further being sub-divided into smaller ones, slightly differing from one another. Sufism was not free from this contagion, rather it was adding to the speed with which the Muslim world was hastening to its doom. In the next chapter we shall, therefore, try to ascertain the causes that led to this degeneration and disintegration.

CHAPTER VI.

THE THEORY OF THE UNITY OF GOD AND SPIRITUAL EXCELLENCES.

The development of Sufi doctrines was accelerated by the degeneration of the Islāmic spirit and of social unity. Islāmic society at this time was characterised by anarchy in politics, in philosophy, in science and in theology. There sprang up systems each inconsistent with and contradictory to another. The spirit of discord and dissension ran high. The early thinkers, who had never dreamt of founding new orders or sects, were placed at the head of these orders, and were held in great veneration. Many new movements were started by the politically ambitious or discontented persons and, in order to gain popularity, they falsely associated themselves with the names of reformers and saints who were nothing but sincere Muslims. The unity of the Islāmic society was being threatened and very few people were sanguine about its continuity or revival. The idea of an Islāmic brotherhood was slowly breaking up and giving place to racial, local, geographical and territorial considerations and it is a strange coincidence, that all this was happening at the time when the theory of nationality on the basis of territorialism was fast spreading and gaining a foothold in the western world.

The reasons for this disintegration of the Muslim society are not far to seek. The energy of the Arab race in the domain of politics and militarism had almost been exhausted. The reaction was evident. It did not take long to appear. The Arabic-speaking nations had imbibed a spirit of Greek philosophy. They had given up the system of government which was introduced by Caliph 'Umar I. For instance, Arabs began to acquire lands against the injunctions laid down by the same Caliph, who intended them to be a military race. The natural consequence was that when they settled in other countries, their patriotism for their mother-land was considerably weakened.

The means adopted by the wreckers of Islāmic social integrity were chiefly religious, though the real causes were political grievances particularly against the ascendancy of the Arab race. The first step in this direction was taken by giving a new interpretation of the Qur'ān, Sunnah, and other institutions associated with Islām.[1] The persons who were chiefly involved in this movement were the 'Alids,[2] the believers in the succession and Imāmat of 'Alī, the cousin and son-in-law of the prophet. The Qur'ān and Sunnah were silent about the matter, otherwise the early followers of the prophet would not have disobeyed such clear and

---

1 Nicholson: Literary History of the Arabs, p. 392.

2 Ibn Khaldūn: Muqaddimah, p. 472, 473 (Beyrout Ed. 1900 A.D.); cf. Macdonald: Muslim Theology, pp. 18, 19.

important commands if there were any. Then there was the accomplished fact of the Khilāfat of Abū Bakr, 'Umar and 'Uthmān, a fact that has always been regarded with extreme respect and reverence by the vast majority of Muslims. The 'Alids, who were chiefly of Persian origin, had risen against the ruling power now and then, but without much success. They tried to find out a new method of achieving their object. A new interpretation of Islām must be given and since no ordinary meanings of the letter of the Qur'ān could yield conclusions which they wanted to preach, they tried to derive them through mystic interpretation of the text. But this could be done without betraying the mischief involved, only in the case of a few verses, for the rest could not yield to this far-fetched method of misconstruction. Therefore clear verses were left alone, while the others were stretched to an absurd length of misinterpretation. This method was imitated by other Sufis, who wanted to establish the super-human and divine superiority of their spiritual guides. It is significant, that all Sufi orders originate with 'Alī. There is only one solitary exception of a Sufi order called Naqshbandī, which claims to originate with Abū Bakr instead of 'Alī and the theories and practices followed by its supporters are much more Islāmic than those of the other orders. This fact leads us to suppose that the real motive of the introduction of

Sufism among the Muslims at this stage was to enlist support for the claims of 'Alī's descendants to Khilāfat.

Then there was Greek philosophy which was making rapid progress in the Islāmic world.[1] After a few of its books were translated into Arabic, it began to mould and modify the beliefs and thoughts of the learned section. On account of its comprehensiveness and rationality it was rapidly growing as the ideal of all thinking and reasoning people. Muslim theologians were baffled by the logic of the Greek thought. This campaign against orthodox theology was led by the Mu'tazilites. But very soon the theologians learnt by experience, that the best way to fight against the evil was to adopt the weapons of their opponents. So they slowly began to assimilate the principles of Greek philosophy in their interpretation of the Qur'ān and Sunnah. Al-'Ashari and his followers led the opposition.

Out of the ancient Greek philosophers it was Aristotle who was chiefly studied as an authority. It was due to this fact that specialisation in different branches of learning continued among the Arabs, for Aristotle was the first to classify different branches of knowledge. The western movement of Neo-Platonism had also begun to spread with rapidity and enthusiasm. Plato had begun to be studied with the object that his

1 Nicholson : Literary History of the Arabs, p. 388.

arguments might be opposed to those of the philosophers who mainly depended upon the authority of Aristotle. Plato, particularly as represented by Neo-Platonism, supplied a good deal of material for mysticism. The name of Plato became current in Islāmic literature as the type and ideal of a mystic philosopher. Commentaries of the Qur'ān were written in the light of Greek philosophy.[1] Most of the theories of that philosophy have been exploded by recent researches, but to give an interpretation against those commentaries which were written on the assumption of the truth of those theories is still considered a heresy by a section of the learned Muslims.

This raised a very important and controversial question about the interpretation of the Qur'ān. The best opinion about the subject appears to be of those who hold that since the prophet belonged to Mecca and to the Quraish, the language of the Qur'ān must be construed strictly according to the idiom and usage of the Quraish.[2] There are certain passages in the Holy Book that cannot be understood unless their historical origin is clearly grasped. It is generally agreed that some verses of the Qur'ān are explained by others. Again, the Qur'ān has used many ordinary words in a technical sense of its own, a sense in which they were never

1 Of such Commentaries, one written by Fakhru'd-dīn Rāzī has become classic.

2 Bukhārī: Ṣaḥīḥ, Manāqib Quraish.

used before and which can be understood only by comparing their use in various contexts, and by keeping in mind the general object of the book, which was the moral reformation of humanity. Certain verses can be understood only with reference to the beliefs, usages and customs prevalent among the Arabs which according to Islām had only crept among them because they had neglected their gospels. Certain other verses are allegorical, and still others lay down general principles abstracted out of individual occurrences in the days of the prophet.

The Sufis disregarded all these rules of interpretation and tried to explain the verses in a mystical and allegorical sense, giving a new meaning to almost all the technical terms like Heaven, Hell, Angels and even God. The description of Heaven and Hell in the Qur'ān was perhaps meant to be literal but the Sufis interpreted them in the terms of pleasure and displeasure of God.

With the change in the conception of Heaven and Hell there came a change in the meaning of all those things that were associated in the Qur'ān with these objects of reward and punishment. The pure wine of heaven came to mean Divine love and thenceforward the word wine came to symbolize the Love of God.[1] This mystic use of the word

---

1 Mark the following lines of Nizāmi:

مرا ساقي از وعدهٔ ایزدی ست صبوح از خرابی ی از بیخودي ست

Continued on the next page.

wine has been overdone by the later Sufi writers, specially by Persian poets of Sufi tendencies. It looks strange that even moral poets like Sa'dı could not rise above the tendencies of their age, concerning the usage of this term. Probably its use in their age had become so common that a departure from it would have offended the literary sense of that age.

Unity of Existence (Pantheism), Unity of Reflection, and Unity of Creation.

Another feature of the time was that Persian ideas, which had so far remained in abeyance on account of the overwhelming influence of the Arab intellect, now began to assert themselves in Sufi literature.[1] The Aryan Pantheism combined with a similar theory of Plotinus developed into the famous Sufi doctrine of the Unity of Existence. It was a fusion of the Islāmic Unity of God, of the universal Spirit (Brahamātmā) theory of the Aryans, and the Greek conception of the Unity of existing reality. No doubt, the Islāmic conception of Divine Unity dominated but in place of the Unity of a Personal God, as Islām had conceived it to be, it was now only an abstract unity involving plurality

---

می کو چو آبِ زلال آمده ست بہر چار مذھب حلال آمده ست

می کاصل مذھب بدو شد تمام نه آن می که آمد بمذھب حرام

cf. wine odes (Khamrıyya) by Ibnu'l-Fāriḍ, a part of which has been translated by Prof. Nicholson in his Studies in Islamic Mysticism, pp. 183-184; also see 'Umar Khayyām's Rubā'iyyāt.

1 O'Leary: Arabic Thought, p. 192.

in its content and individuality only in name and as an attribute.

This doctrine was clearly stated by the famous western Sufi writer Muḥyu'ddīn ibnu'l-'Arabī. He was credited with saintship of a high order by the Sufis and was called ash-Shaikhu'l-Akbar[1] for the only reason, that he was the first writer to give a systematic exposition of the theory, and to support it on philosophic grounds.[2] References to it were found in the writings of early Sufi thinkers, but they were rare and casual. Ibnu'l-'Arabī in his exposition of the theory is avowedly more a student of Greek philosophy than a true Sufi. He professes to justify it on Islāmic grounds, but a very cursory perusal of his works is sufficient to convince that his treatment of the subject is beset with all the weaknesses of the ancient Greek philosophy and that the connection between the theory and the Islāmic principles upon which he tries to base it is very weak. But his attempt is commendable, so far as he has given an intelligible philosophic form to the vague tendencies of his contemporary Sufis. On the whole the attempt appears to have been a failure, the reasons of

---

1 Nicholson: Literary History of the Arabs, p. 404.

2 Mujaddid Aḥmad Sirhindī: Letters, Vol. I. Letter 272; also see Jāmī: Nafaḥātu'l-Uns, p. 633.

A clear exposition of Ibnu'l-'Arabī's doctrines is found in 'Abdu'r-Razzāq's (d. 730 A.H.) Commentary of Ibnu'l-'Arabī's writings. He clearly stated Ibnu'l-'Arabī's positions with regard to the Unity but disagreed with him about the freedom of Divine Will.

which are not far to seek. As soon as philosophic grounds were found for the theory it lost all its charm for those who were more inclined towards orthodox Islām than towards Sufism. They recoiled from a belief, which, they now began to consider, was dragging them towards the worst possible heresy. A section of the more religious Sufis broke away from it. Ibnu'l-'Arabi's treatment made it popular among the Sufis, but at the same time it created an opposition in the camp.[1]

Moreover, the theory while extending the scope of love among human beings at large, weakened the bond of love and sympathy among the Muslims as a class. According to this theory there was no fundamental distinction between believers and un-believers, and the former therefore, had no reason to prefer their brethren in faith over the others. Thus in view of this theory all human beings are equal without any regard to their distinct faith, creed, nationality, locality or blood. Islām itself had levelled all distinctions of nationality, locality and blood, but it had emphasised the distinction between belief and unbelief[2] and between good and bad.[3] Even this was brushed aside by this theory of the Unity of Existence as

1 See the writings of Ash-Sha'rānī of Cairo (d. 973) who, while professing to defend Ibnu'l-'Arabī, completely broke away from him with regard to the theory of Unity; also Ibn Taymiya's writings who protested against saint-worship in any form.

2 The Qur'ān LXVIII. 35 and XXXII. 18.

3 *Ibid.* XLI. 34.

accepted by the Sufis. By weakening the bond of sympathy and love among the Muslims, it made them so much unfit as rulers, for this bond of love is an indispensable condition for the continuation of the supremacy of the rulers over the ruled. It is only so long as the rulers consider themselves superior to the ruled that they can control their subjects and can legitimately claim to administer their affairs. One of the devices which the ruled nations usually adopt to overthrow the ascendancy of their rulers is to claim the right of equality with them, and to establish this right the general principle, that all human beings are equal, is of great help. The Persians had this object in view when they caught hold of this theory as a means to weaken the force of the Arab rule over them.

Besides, this doctrine is inconsistent with the moral feelings of responsibility.[1] If both the good and bad are in God then there is no essential difference between the two. No doubt this view would extend our toleration, but at the cost of finer feelings of intolerance of evil. Toleration of the weaknesses of others is a creditable element in one's character, but if it tends to wash away all instinctive horror of evil and obscure one's judgment of discrimination between the moral rightness and

---

1 O'Leary: Arabic Thought, p. 199. Also mark the following verse of 'Aṭṭār, p. 587 (Works of 'Aṭṭār, Nawalkishore Press):

همه از تست اینجا چه بد و نیك ولی ما خون ریزان در این ریگ

wrongness then it may end in depriving a person of all his moral sense and power of ethical judgment.

Again, if all creatures are equal, if human beings and animals are equal, and the animals admittedly have no sense of moral responsibility, then surely human beings as well have no such responsibility.[1] The whole poetry of 'Umar Khayyām and other writers who do not believe in the moral responsibility of human beings is the natural development of this phase of the doctrine.[2] The Qur'ān had distinguished human beings from the rest of the creation on account of their possession of the attribute of moral responsibility. It says, "Surely We offered the trust (moral responsibility) to the heavens and earth and the mountains, but they refused to bear it and shrank from it, but man bore it."[3]

Probably all these developments of the theory were not anticipated by writers like Ibnu'l-'Arabī, otherwise they would have shrunk from it in great horror. In all probability they intended to make

---

1 'Aṭṭār: Mathnawī, Ilāhī-Nāma, p. 798, Maqāla Thāniya, Story I (Nawalkishore Press). How the theory of unity as conceived by Sufis takes away the distinction between men and animals and good and bad.

2 Mark the following lines of 'Umar Khayyām (Rubā'iyyāt-i-Khayyām, Anwār-i-Ahmadi Press, Allahabad, 299):

در ملك تو از طاعت من هیچ فزود ؟   و ز معصیتی که رفت نقصانی بود ؟
چون کار نه بر مراد ما خواهد بود   اندیشه و جهد ما کجا دارد سود ؟

And also see Rubā'ī No. 632 which expresses a similar idea.

3 The Qur'ān XXXIII. 72.

it only a working hypothesis for the solution of cosmogonical and cosmological problems. The problems which it purported to solve were borrowed from Greek philosophers on the one hand and from the Indian systems of philosophy on the other.

The Greeks conceived the question purely from the point of view of scientific interest and stated it thus, "How was the world created? Of what stuff was it made? How was it sustained and whither was it going?" Such cosmological problems were the first to engage the attention of the ancient Greek philosophers.

After sometime we find that the current of Greek thought was turned inward. With the advent of Sophists and after them with Socrates and Plato, man became the chief object of philosophic enquiry. Henceforward among the Greeks, the philosophic problems circle round humanity and human activity rather than round the world and its creation. Man became the measure of everything.

It was at this stage that Islām took up the problem. It had raised humanity above the rest of the creation. It had announced that God had created the rest of the creatures to serve human beings,[1] who were the vicars of God on earth.[2] Therefore, the question before the Muslims was: what is the relation between God, the Creator and

1 The Qur'ān XLV. 13. 2 *Ibid.* II. 30.

man, the creature? Ḥallāj had cried out that he was the Truth, meaning thereby that a human being could advance to such an extent that there remained no difference between God and man, that one became inseparably intermingled with the other. It was in this sense that many after him understood the phrase Merger in God or Fanā-fi'llāh, or the Ḥulūl as it is more technically called by Sufis. But as it was completely against the spirit of Islām, Hallāj was decreed to death by the orthodox theologians. Islām had given a sort of dualistic explanation of the problem of creation. It had laid down that no creature, however high it might rise in progress, could ever become at one with the Creator. According to Islām the Creator and the creatures remained eternally different realities. Even the apostles, though the most perfect of creatures, ever remained humble slaves to the Creator, content with the humble dignity of prophethood.

But this dualistic hypothesis about the cosmological problem, did not very much appeal to the theoretical tendencies of the Aryans, though it had worked tolerably well with the Arabs. The gap was there, and the weakness of the explanation evident. If there be two realities, eternally different from each other, the question as to how the existence of the world in general and that of humanity in particular is to be connected with the more original and more fundamental reality, that of God, remains unanswered. How and why God created the world is briefly the crucial objection against this dualistic view. Either a dead matter should be posed as eternally co-existing side by side with God Himself, which explanation was given by Vedanta philosophy in India and Peripatetic school in Greece, or the world was an emanation from God. The later alternative was accepted by Ibnu'l-'Arabī and others of his cast of mind, since the solution given by Vedanta philosophy placed the Unity of God in a doubtful position. For if matter existed eternally side by side with God then it must be deified as well, inasmuch as it possessed the attribute of eternity, an essential distinguishing characteristic of Divinity.

The Sufis had learnt from Islām that there was no God but one, and therefore the only way to explain the diversity of existence consistently with this Unity was to conceive the diversity as so many different forms of existence of one reality called God. They quote in support of their hypothesis a well-known verse of the Qur'ān, "Every moment He is in a (different) state (of glory)."[1] This solution of the cosmological problem saved them from falling into Polytheism while it satisfied the difficulties of the problem.

It is not, therefore, quite correct to say that the principle of "Unity of Existence" or panthe-

---

1 The Qur'ān LV. 29.

ism leads its believers to polytheism as it was really conceived to save the believers from this very pitfall. This doctrine claims to satisfy and make a sort of compromise between two diverse, and to some extent inconsistent, views that the existence or reality is really one or many. Whether the reality is one or more than one was the question whose definite solution finally decided either for or against the theory of the Unity of Existence. Islām had not passed any conclusive judgment upon the subject, and it was right in doing so, since any definite expression of opinion with regard to its solution, might have made it unacceptable for the believers in the opposite view. Islām had refrained from passing any definite judgment upon astronomical, cosmological and strictly philosophical controversies, that did not fall within the province of its moral, spiritual and social reformation. It was for a similar reason that Islām had not discussed the question of creation elaborately. It was this question which the theory of the Unity of Existence purported to answer.

Howevermuch some of us might wish that Islām should have given a conclusive and definite solution of these problems, its attitude in such cases was uniform and clear. It left a wide scope, as already pointed out, for independent opinion and free thinking. It was slow in giving any definite explanation of such questions which were not concerned with the scope which it had appropriated to itself. The boundaries of this scope are very difficult for many to understand. It may clear the difficulty, to some extent, if we point out that the province which Islām had appropriated to itself was primarily concerned with the question, "how to live well?" It primarily touched those habits of action and thought which were directly and intimately connected with living well. It had systematically avoided the expression of binding opinions about questions of purely scientific interest. The founder of Islām probably well understood, that theories in sciences were ever changing, and therefore formulation of one fixed opinion in such matters would make Islām unacceptable to a large section of humanity.

But even the phrase, living well, could in a wider sense cover almost all the activities of existence. Therefore, among the requirements of living well a distinction was made between those activities essentially related to human life and those that applied purely to animal or vegetative life. About the former activities, it was the first business of Islām to lay down binding rules of conduct, while with regard to the latter which were regarded of comparatively smaller importance, it had left every individual free to choose a course for himself according to the need of time and circumstances.

Nevertheless, Islām laid down sometimes a command, and very often an advice for some of these unessential activities. It distinguished the essential from the unessential activities of life. The notion about the essential and non-esentia1 activities and requirements of life is usually changing with the change of time and age, therefore, led by modern notions of essential requirements of life, we might consider some commands of Islām to be trifling. Prof. Nicholson, in his "Studies of Islamic Mysticism," points out how some of the Sufis rigidly followed the prophet even in using the tooth-pick after meals as a regular habit, and considered it a very pious deed.[1] The illustration is unfortunate because the command of using the tooth-pick cannot be traced in the Qur'ān, but it very well supports my statement. Moreover, it is to be remembered that when Islām was in the formation, there was no clear line of demarcation between religion and other practical sciences like hygiene and medicine. Therefore, though systematically refraining from touching the field of theoretical sciences and from announcing authoritative theories, it touched sometimes in very minute details the practical aspects of human activities. Islām itself considers one set of activities and beliefs as merely permitted but not essential; therefore, it would be easier to understand Islām if we differentiate between the modern notions of essential requirements of life and Islāmic notions about the same.

---

1 Nicholson: Studies in Islāmic Mysticism, p. 47.

It is an admitted fact that certain elements in human nature are comparatively constant, while the others are changeable. History tells us that certain factors in human nature have been found existing since its very creation.

Again there are certain passions of the human soul that are found common in all the human beings, irrespective of place, climate, environment or any other circumstances. Islām has tried to appeal to and to regulate such universal elements of human nature. But it chiefly prescribes rules for moulding one's life according to a certain standard, which can generally be attained without the help of external circumstances, for it really depends upon searching the depths of one's own soul. The process is internal and consists in exertion of the active aspect of human nature.

Coming to the real point at issue, this theory of the Unity of Existence claimed to be a solution of a cosmological problem which was borrowed from Greek philosophers and it was intended to bridge a gap which the Islāmic solution of the problem was thought to have made. Outwardly it satisfied the craving of the Aryan mind for polytheistic incarnation, but in reality it was intended to avoid any such implications. It was calculated to prove fatal for the Arab rule, and therefore on this ground it was hailed and popularised by the ruled nations, particularly Persians. It weakened the sense of responsibility inherent in human nature, and levelled all distinctions between man and man and even between man and animals.

This view has been called pantheism by western writers on Muslim Theology and Mysticism. It may be a form of pantheism, but it is not pantheism in that sense in which it is used in modern philosophy. I have already pointed out, in the last chapter, that the abstract unity of God as opposed to the relational and concrete Unity, was fast becoming the fundamental Sufi creed. This doctrine of the Unity of Existence was a natural development of the abstract Unity of God. In the case of abstract Unity the conception of Unity was limited to the person of God alone, considered independent of any relationship, the creatures being regarded as connected with Him only through the bond of love and obedience. In the case of the Unity of Existence the conception of Unity enveloped the whole of creation in it. The difference between the two is evident. In the former case the question is theological, while in the latter it is cosmological and metaphysical. The former is concerned with the problem of the nature and essence of God, while the latter is concerned with the question of the Universe. This development clearly indicates the overwhelming influence of Greek philosophy in the latter case. The problem had in this process of development really changed from theological to cosmological. According to this view, God is ultimate reality from which various forms of reality proceed and beget their existence.

Thus we see that this theory is calculated to solve the cosmological as well as the metaphysical problem. It professes to explain not only the creation of the universe, but also the nature of reality. The world in view of this theory is not grossly material, but has a predominating spiritual element inseparably connected with it at the heart of things. But for this spiritual aspect, it should have been akin to Spinoza's metaphysical theory of pantheism, wherein metaphysical or mechanical aspects of it are more prominent.

In the universe we experience phenomena of two kinds. Things possess certain common characters, but each individual thing differs from the rest of the created things. Thus there is both unity and diversity palpably present. The doctrine of the unity of existence lays stress upon the common characters of things and asserts that they alone are real and constitute their real essence. Since they are possessed in common by all things therefore all things are essentially the same, though they might be accidentally different. Now names are given to things on account of certain accidental reasons, and therefore things differ in names. Thus the solution comes to this, that unity is real while diversity is only apparent. Individual attributes and names represent the accidental in things, while the substance of all things which makes those things what they really are is the same, and that substance is named God.

Evidently the theory is not Islāmic. Islām had left the nature of ultimate reality undiscussed. It not only did not discuss it but positively discouraged such discussions. Islām should have abhorred it on the apparent ground that it destroyed the fundamental distinction between good and evil. Islām had postulated good and evil as two separate realities[1] concerned with the human conduct, and not as two phases of godhead as the Persian religion had done. If the things essentially proceeded from God then both good and evil were caused by Him alone, and thus there was no reason for His being called the source of goodness. Islām had laid down the principle that though both came into existence by God's order, yet one was from God and the other was on account of the weaknesses of human nature.[3]

Moreover, it did violence to Islāmic sentiment that a Muslim was always to regard himself a servant of God. It was regarded by Islām as the climax of human progress, that a creature should consider himself as an obedient and humble servant of his Creator. If there was no fundamental difference between him and God, between good and evil, then why all this labour and toil of obeying the law and serving God and humanity[3]?

---

1 The Qur'ān XLI. 34. 2 *Ibid.* XXX. 36.
3 Nicholson : Studies in Islāmic Mysticism, pp. 61, 62.

It is evident, therefore, that this hypothesis was beset with certain weaknesses which could not be defended on any grounds. With a view to avoid them Mujaddid Aḥmad Sirhindī advocated and expounded another principle which he called the "Unity of Reflection."[1] This principle was more Islāmic, more spiritual and indeed was less objectionable on the grounds of fundamental tenets of Islām.

This theory like that of the "Unity of Existence" was intended to solve the cosmological problem of creation and of the relationship of the creator and creatures. Briefly stated the theory was this, that the creator and the created were both real though different in their essence. One was real in its essence while the other was real as the reflection of the other. The created things were real so far as they reflected the reality of the Infinite. They were real more or less in proportion to the clearness of the reflection of the reality of their creator. Thus reality itself was classified. The measure and grade of the reflection determined the reality of each created thing. The diversity existed and played an important part in the universe, but all the created things had a uniform nature so far as they all reflected the same ultimate reality of the Creator.

When critically examined this theory appears

---

1 Mujaddid Aḥmad Sirhindī: Letters, Vol. I. Letters 43, 160, 234.

to be more satisfactory for an orthodox Islāmic mind than that of the Unity of Existence. It should be remembered that among the Muslim Sufis there were a number of persons of extremely orthodox views. Islām, as I have pointed out above, never conceived of raising the creatures to the level of the Creator under any circumstances. This theory never thought of filling the chasm that Islām had created between God and human beings. Human soul might progress even so far as to talk with its Creator, but it ever remained a distinct entity. The vague notions of the merger of human soul into that of God, that were borrowed from the Aryans, specially of the Indian stock, were totally unknown to the founder of Islām or to the early Muslims. This theory distinguished the Creator from creatures still more sharply. The reflection of the reality was real, since it was associated with reality, but it was not a part of the Creator as one substance is a part of another substance. The relation between the reflection and the real thing may be that of dependence of the one upon the other, but it was not the same relationship as between the part and the whole in any sense.

Apart from the fact that this theory was more satisfactory than that of Ibnu'l-'Arabi on orthodox grounds, it was more sound even philosophically. It satisfied the demands of both kinds of our experiences, of unity as well as of diversity, while the other theory sacrificed diversity in order to satisfy the demands of unity. This hypothesis, therefore, was more scientific, and of wider application. The supporters of the former theory had to explain certain phenomena on the basis of analogy, while this theory dispensed with such explanation, by giving a real character both to the Creator and the creatures.

This theory was also more satisfactory from the cosmological standpoint. It gave an explanation for both the sides of the problem. It established a relationship between two real things. The former theory had lost sight of one side of the question while giving undue importance at least in name to the other. But this theory gave a relation between two realities, while in the case of the other, there arose no question of relationship, since out of the two concepts involved, one was arbitrarily taken as non-real. When we ask how the universe is created by God, it implies one fact very clearly that at least for the time being the Creator and the creatures exist as two different things. The theory paid due consideration to both the sides, while the other considered facts related of one side alone as real.

Moreover, this theory left the fundamental distinction between good and evil quite intact. The good was an attribute of the real. It belonged to the creatures so far as they were images of the real. In short, according to this theory, good proceeded from God, and evil from the creatures, so far as they were different from the source of all good, the highest of realities. Evil was due to the limitations of our nature.

This theory also helped to explain a principle of orthodox Islām that creatures were good in proportion to the depth of relationship which existed between them and their Creator. The better a creature represented and reflected the reality, the more of good it possessed. The Qur'ān had laid down that belief was the essential condition of being able to perform good deeds. According to it, the deeds of those who performed them without being believers, were like sowing seeds in the scanty soil of a rock, which was in danger of being swept off by a slight shower of rain.[1] Belief was the necessary foundation on which character could be built, and belief alone could clean the heart of a man and prepare it to receive the light, or revelation of God. In this way this theory explained those verses that enjoined the believers to approach God with a clean and upright heart.[2] Rūmī meant this when he said, "Even if thy heart is opaque like iron, (the only way to purify it is to) cleanse it over and over again."[3]

Students of philosophy can well understand, how far this theory is akin to the Monad theory of Leibnitz, though not quite identical to it. It is

1 The Qur'ān II. 264.

2 *Ibid.* XXVI. 89 and XXXVII. 84.

3 همچو آهن گرچه تیره هیکلی — صیقلی کن صیقلی کن صیقلی

beset, therefore, with all the difficulties of that theory or of any other theory which takes up diversity as real side by side with unity. Diversity is a great labyrinth, of which it is difficult to come out if once you fall into it. The reason is twofold. Firstly, it is difficult to co-ordinate such a vast number of diverse facts, except on the basis of some universal principle. When once you seek the help of some unifying principle, it appropriates the whole field of facts and becomes an all important element in the theory. Thus all the theories that accept diversity as real, sooner or later pass imperceptibly into some form of unity. The theory of the Unity of reflection was no exception. It had started with the assumption that diversity was real but it concluded with evolving a principle that the quality of an individual thing was to be fixed by its capacity to represent or reflect the real. Even according to this view logically interpreted individual creatures have no reality, except so far as they reflect the one fundamental reality of God. Secondly, the only way to understand diversity is to unify the diverse elements under one principle. In order that different facts might become parts of our system of knowledge, they must be unified and grouped. Thus, in order to become a part of our knowledge they must lose their existence as independent and different facts. Therefore in hypothesizing on facts in the domain of any science, we must neglect diversity to a great extent. But no science can be possible without individual facts and diverse phenomena. Therefore we should attach due importance to each of the two aspects of our experience, (that is, diversity and unity) and this is done by this theory to a certain extent.

This theory possesses another great weakness. It implies that there are different grades of reality. One thing, according to it, can be more real than the other. If everything borrows its existence from another, which is truly real and is the condition and source of all reality, then this latter thing must possess reality as well as something of unreality, since both these aspects are found in the former. This conclusion at once involves us into two absurdities, one, that there exists something which is unreal, a conclusion to which the supporters of this theory would never agree to subscribe, and secondly, that a thing can at the same time, possess two contradictory attributes of reality and unreality as in this case.

Moreover, the idea of gradation in reality is not appealing to a scientific mind. "Reality is one, unclassable, indestructible and uniform," says every student of science.

Again, this theory does not tell us anything about the nature of reality. What is reality? is not the question which it contemplates to reply. This question has not been satisfactorily answered by any theory that assumes diversity and difference as real. It may satisfy a cosmological and theological enquirer but cannot satisfy a student of metaphysics.

But we can say that all such theories that involve intricate metaphysics and cosmological questions have not been congenial to the spirit of Islām. It was silent on purely scientific questions, therefore, it did not very much encourage to take up such questions under the cloak of religion. We can say that as a Sufi doctrine dealing with the question of the relationship of human soul with God, this theory was far more Islāmic and ethical than the former one, though less metaphysical and probably less scientific.

As opposed to both these views, the unity preached by Islām was the unity of the Personality of God as an object of worship. The principle for which the prophet had fought all his life was an answer to the question whether any other being, excepting God, was the fit object of worship. Evidently, therefore, the prophet had approached the question purely from the theological point of view. When we realise that according to Islām the person who worships anything or being beside Allāh shall never be pardoned, the point becomes still clearer. The problem of creation was merely taken up as a side issue to establish that God alone was the fit object of human worship and adoration. Thus, according to Islām, the problem of creation was a secondary problem. The solution offered for the cosmological problem thus raised was a sort of "Unity of creation."[1] The only attribute which was found common in all things was that they were created and brought into existence by One Infinite Personality. Besides this common element in the nature of things, Islām does not press for any other common principle to be believed. Among the created beings, of course, there is very perceptible difference between human beings and all other creatures, which Islām particularly emphasises. The former are created to rule the rest of creation, chiefly for two reasons; firstly, because it is the only creation capable of knowledge, especially the knowledge that is possible through language and revelation,[2] and secondly, because this creation alone is capable of moral responsibility, which the rest of the creation refused to accept.[3] Knowledge is serviceable because it helps us to discriminate between good and bad, right and wrong.

After marking this distinction between the two kinds of creation, one of which is created to serve the other, while the other to rule the rest, the Qur'ān points out that it is highly derogatory to the position and sublimity of human

1 Waḥdat-i-Takhlīq, as opposed to the two rival theories discussed above, Waḥdat-i-Wujūd by Ibnu'l-'Arabī and Waḥdat-i-Shūhūd by Mujaddid Aḥmad Sirhindī.

2 The Qur'ān II. 33 and 38. 3 *Ibid.* XXIII. 72.

beings to worship, adore or serve any being other than the Creator, Who has granted this lofty position to them. From here begins the subject-matter proper of the teachings of Islām, which purported to bring about a moral and spiritual reformation among the human beings. It is clear from this that according to Islām there are three kinds of realities the relation of which is to be correctly established. God is the Eternal, Infinite, Beneficient and Merciful Creator of everything. Man is His special and favourite creation, created to govern the rest of creation but to serve Him alone. Other creatures besides man, resemble him only in being created by the same Creator. It is on account of this bond that I have given this theory the name of "Unity of creation." But they do not possess the qualities of knowledge, revelation and moral responsibility, whose possession have made man a favourite creation. These qualities while making man a ruler of all creation have made his life full of misery and devoid of peace and rest. Human life has become rich but at the cost of peace. It is in this richness of contents of life that man's greatness consists. From the view that Islām holds about human nature it can be safely inferred that it never contemplated to explain reality by an Abstract Unity, a dull exclusion of diversity. Reality is full of diversity. The greater the diversity in the contents of a thing the greater the reality in it as illustrated in human life. But Islām did not draw any such logical inferences. As I have said above, it did not propose to discuss the nature of reality, or the ultimate nature of anything, excepting that of human beings which was its chief theme. It kept quiet over all abstruse problems of theoretical nature, which had no direct bearing on human life. Thus we can safely say that Islām did neither conceive the theory of the Unity of Existence, nor that of the Unity of Reflection. The fundamental postulate of the Unity of God which was so vehemently pressed by the prophet was intended to emphasise only the Unity of God as an object of worship, veneration, devotion and service,[1] and the theory of the unity of creation was only taken up to serve as a proof for this view. This fact becomes quite clear if we analyse the Muslim Logos (Kalimah), "Lā'ilāha, illa'llāhu". It means, "There is no being, fit to be an object of worship excepting one Allāh." Allāh, in the Arabic usage, is considered to be an existential name of the person of God, while Ilāh is the attribute for anything that is taken as an object of worship or adoration, according to him who takes it as such.[2] It is clear from the form of this Logos that it is not the existence of diverse things which is denied, but that they are devoid of the attribute of Ilāh. The existence of two grades of creation, man and all other things, Islām rather takes for granted and bases its arguments on their existence but denies eternity to

1 Mujaddid Aḥmad Sirhindī : Letters, Vol. I. Letter 272.

2 Lane's Lexicon under اله.

any one of them. They will all perish and nothing beside Allāh will continue to exist eternally.[1] Thus things, according to Islām, do possess existence but a temporary one. This again leads us to a consideration similar to that of the Unity of Reflection, whose philosophic value we have already judged.

The Logos or Kalimah of Islām has emphasised this attribute of Allāh because it is through this attribute, that a relationship can be established between Him and His creatures particularly human beings. The Qur'ān says, "And I have not created the jinn and the men except that they should worship Me."[2] The question may still be asked about the reality and nature of God as a Person. The two theories of the Unity of Existence and Unity of Reflection, which we have discussed above, particularly the first, purport to give an answer to this question by proposing to establish a Unity in the nature of God. In this Unity they include the whole diversity of the visible and perceptible world. Maulānā Jāmī in the introduction to his famous book Nafaḥātu'l-Uns has mentioned four kinds of Unity: the unity of faith, the unity of knowledge, the unity of Ecstasy and the unity of His Existence. By the first he means that unity which is the essential foundation of faith, that is the unity of God, as the only object of worship, which I have shown above is implied

1 The Qur'ān LV. 26, 27. 2 *Ibid.* LI. 65.

in the Muslim Logos and is the only kind of unity conceived and established by Islām. By the second he understands that kind of belief in the mind of the believer by which he should feel and regard Allāh alone as the real and absolute cause of all movements, changes, actions and existences. The third kind indicates that the believer should begin to realise within him the presence of the light whose source he should regard to be Allāh only, even as the moon and the stars are deemed to reflect the light of the sun, the only source of visible light. At this stage the believer begins not only to have faith as in the first stage, and not only knowledge as in the second stage, but also to feel within himself the light and the reflection of the attributes of Allāh. This form represents the theory of Unity as presented by Mujaddid Aḥmad Sirhindī which we have already discussed in detail. Finally comes the true unity of the nature and person of Allāh, the Unity of Existence as presented by Ibnu'l-'Arabī and others. This also we have discussed above in detail, and found it wanting in many ways both from the philosophical and theological points of view. Jāmī seems to have thought that these are the different stages of belief in Unity through which a seeker has to pass during his progress. According to this order, the Unity of God as an object of worship is the lowest stage and and is just the starting threshold of spiritual progress; while as already pointed out, Islām really established and emphasised only the first kind of Unity and discussed the second only as far as it was necessary to prove and establish the first. The third kind may be said to be not quite subversive of the fundamental Islāmic principles, so far as it can be inferred and deduced from the first two. Islām is quite silent about the fourth kind and there is no indication or sign in the Qur'ān or genuine traditions which may suggest that it was ever conceived much less preached by the founder of Islām. This kind of theory, therefore, was a pure innovation and, as I have suggested above, was the result of Persian, Indian, and Greek influences.

Maulānā Jāmi and others of his trend of mind have made a grave mistake in understanding the real object of Islām. Their tendency of mind appears to suggest as if the object of Islām was to lay the foundation of a school for specialisation in spiritualism. Probably a similar mistake was made by the doctors of law who spent their whole life and energy in bringing out and evolving nice codes and systems of law out of simple Qur'ānic injunctions. Islām neither really intended to lay down the foundation of schools of research in spiritualism nor in jurisprudence but after laying down certain general principles of universal nature for the guidance of human life, it proposed to leave every individual free to develop his personality to its highest extent. It gave general law so far as was essential for this purpose, but it wanted to make the foundation of human activity spiritual, because this was the only way of giving life a serious turn and of making the reformation useful and permanent. Therefore it placed that attribute of Allāh, which was directly concerned with human beings, in the forefront and treated His other attributes so far as they were helpful in establishing this one on a firm footing. It positively discouraged all discussion about the ultimate nature of abstruse subjects like soul, God and other things which are not directly concerned with the question of human reformation.

We now pass on to the consideration of the Sufi doctrine of Excellences and of the valleys or stages of the seeker's spiritual progress.

The Spiritual Excellences.

According to Sufis the human heart (Qalb) is the seat of the idea of God. In mystic terminology it has no association with the physical part of the human organism bearing the same name.[1] It is a spiritual faculty in us, a sort of spiritual sense, something akin to the moral sense as understood by Shaftesbury and others. Sufis consider it a kind of mirror that reflects the reality of God. It is through this faculty that human beings come in touch with their Creator, and it is through this faculty that human beings can progress spiritually, and can draw closer to the fountain of all spiritualism.

1 Al-Ghazālī : al-Munqidh mina'ḍ-ḍalāl.

Sufis divide this progress of the Qalb towards the Infinite into seven stages which are called the spiritual excellences (Latā'if-i-Qalbī).[1] At each stage the faculty begets new characteristics, develops new qualities and acquires new properties. They are (i) Watching the heart (Wuqūf-i-Qalbī), (ii) Watching the number (Wuqūf-i-'Adadī), (iii) Watching the time (Wuqūf-i-Zamanī), (iv) Remembrance (Yād-dāsht), (v) Retirement (Bāz-gasht), (vi) Carefulness (Nigāh-dāsht), (vii) Forgetfulness (Khud-gudhāst). These are the seven stages of the flight of the soul towards its attainment of the object of its love and admiration.[2]

Some Sufi writers have gone even so far as to fix seats in the human body for each of these excellences. But no Sufi of any great repute has given this view any credence. It is similar to the theory of phrenology, which associates passions, emotions, intelligence, reason and other mental faculties with definite physical parts of the brain, and which claims to know the character of a man from the examination of his skull. The fate of this view among the learned Sufis was not different from that of phrenology among the scientists.

---

1 Nicholson : Studies in Islāmic Mysticism, pp. 50-51 ; also see Mujaddid Aḥmad Sirhindī : Letters, Vol. I. Letter 31.

2 Abū 'Alī Fārmadī is said to have been the first Sufi to systematise them. He lived two or three generations before Khwāja Naqshband, who accepted and applied this doctrine for the purpose of training his disciples. See Ḥaqīqatu'l-'Irfān by Abu'l 'Alāi' Faḍlu'd-dīn.

Many famous writers on Sufism repudiate the very idea of excellences and consider them to be a piece of imaginary nonsense,[1] but even those who believe in their existence do not believe them to have any essential association with the physical parts of the heart or the body. Their reasons for this repudiation are clear.

Firstly, the soul is not a material substance; therefore to think that any one of the stages of its progress towards God corresponds to certain physical parts is a meaningless notion. An immaterial thing cannot have material relations and associations.

Secondly, this notion of a material association is likely to cause a good deal of confusion between the two series spiritual and physical, which are independent of one another.

The supporters of this theory say that they give a physical equivalent only to make the notion of the immaterial thing clear. They agree that the soul, its stages of flight, and its goal are all immaterial. But immaterial things can only be grasped through the medium of the perceptible, therefore they give their physical associations simply to enable the seeker to understand their significance.

Even this argument is not strong enough to convince us of the validity of the hypothesis; firstly, because the soul being immaterial has the capacity

---

1 Mujaddid Aḥm ad Sirhindī : Letters, Vol. I. Letter 36.

of grasping a completely immaterial notion, like that of God and mind; secondly, because it is not becoming of truth that for the sake of making it easily conceivable its nature should be changed, and it should be presented to be what it really is not. Truth must exist and shine of its own light and in its own right. If it borrows the right of existence from other things then it does not deserve to be called truth. In the third place such a mode of explaining the reality is very misleading. Some people are likely to misunderstand its very nature. This fact makes the general tendency of mystic interpretation of the Qur'ān and Islām highly objectionable. For instance, according to Sufi authorities the description of Hell and Heaven as given in the Qur'ān is allegorical and is simply intended to stand for some kind of punishment or reward for human actions. But if these things have no real existence then they cannot be expected to appeal to our passions of fear and hope. There could be more effective and more tangible methods of reformation. For instance, the idea of reward or punishment in this world could be more effective if it were more tangible. It is on account of this tendency of Sufis that the more orthodox section of the Muslims does not subscribe to their interpretation.

We can sum up the discussion by saying that the stages through which a soul has to pass during its progress towards God, are not connected with any part of the physical body. They are arbitrary, imaginary and even unreal.[1] Each seeker can classify his experiences differently. To explain them briefly we can say that the heart begins by concentrating its attention upon itself, or in the words of the later Sufis by attending to the attention and influence of the Shaikh, Murshid or spiritual guide. At this stage the heart begins to feel its own existence, and the seeker makes a start by repeating and muttering some Dhikr taught to him by his guide.[2]

The second stage begins with the advanced practice of repeating the name of Allāh according to a fixed number. If the seeker can repeat the Dhikr taught to him by his guide twenty-one times or more in one breath, he becomes fit to be initiated to the third stage. It is to be remembered, however, that at the time when this theory was announced, the personality of the spiritual guide had become indispensable. He leads the seeker through all the stages of spiritual progress. It is easy to see that the individual will has been destroyed, free opinion strangled and the path of the prophet forgotten and neglected.

The third stage is marked with the seeker's rising above time. His conception of God now becomes elevated above and beyond time. For

---

1 Mujaddid Aḥmad Sirhindī : Letters, Vol. I. Letter 36.

2 As an illustration, see Nicholson's Studies in Islāmic Mysticism, p. 5, how Abū Sa'īd began with the repetition of Dhikr taught to him by his Shaikh.

this purpose the guide prescribes certain practices related to imagination and mental vision, which slowly lead him above the limitation of conceiving things in time. In the previous stage he had risen above number, now he ascends even higher than the conception of time. When he once rises above these limitations and weaknesses of human nature, that is number and time, he becomes fit to receive the vision of God.

It is interesting to note that in the philosophy of mysticism number and time are considered to be two categories of human relationship with the external world. They considered them to be two moulds similar to time and space, the moulds of Kant, through which the whole knowledge of the external world was systematised and was made fit to be understood by intellect. They did not believe in any other categories of Kant.

For a mystic, therefore, to transcend number and time had a deeper significance. After concentrating his attention upon his heart at the first stage, he must try to rise higher than the categories of unity and multiplicity and must take the whole existence as one and believe in a kind of pantheism. Number signified to the mystic mind a symbol of separation and diversification. But a seeker must eliminate the distinctions. So he must rise above numbers which represent limitations of human nature. Sufis believed that since intellect was incapable of grasping the whole reality in one vision or in a single mental act, therefore, it had parcelled out reality into so many diverse parts, each of which was represented by a separate number. But a mystic must rise above the process of grasping the reality piecemeal so that it may have an intuition or more technically ecstasy or vision of the One.

The number of 21, as I have already said, was the limit of Dhikr, after which the seeker could be initiated into the third stage. In the Persian language, there happens to be a system of counting, according to which numbers up to twenty are counted separately each having a separate name for itself. After twenty they are counted by adding serial numbers one, two or three. Thus twenty-one is the first number, in the unity, which was separated and divided into so many units, again regains itself, and it is the first number which represents unity through comprising a great deal of diversity under it. It therefore represents the Unity of Existence in a way. The Urdu language also has followed this Persian method of counting separate names for numbers upto twenty and joining two together as one after that. Similar is the case with the English language, wherein it might have been introduced from the same source, though more strictly in English thirteen may stand for the first number in that sense.

Similarly the seeker is not only to go above

the distinctive numbers but also above duration. This distinction of numbers is not only to be overcome in the present but in all duration, in all futures to come. The Unity of Existence is to be regarded as such, through all times and all ages, till the idea of time is completely eliminated.

The fourth stage is that of remembrance, of remembering Him, or realising His reality in one's heart, which has now gone beyond material limitation. This is different from merely muttering His name which was the characteristic of the initial stage.

When thus the disciple begins to realise His attributes in his heart, he must retire from the world. This retirement is not necessarily seclusion, but a sort of mental detachment from worldly things. He should refrain from attaching importance to anything excepting the remembrance of Allāh. He retires from everything but Him, with Whom he is constantly busy at heart. He hears from none but Him, sees none but Him, touches nothing but His reality. From this stage begins abnegation of self (fanā). So far his efforts were directed towards rising above his environment and soaring towards Him, but now he reaches sufficiently near unto Him and slowly begins to merge into God.

When he has attained this stage, the next step he is to take is to be careful in preserving this state of affairs. He must endeavour to perpetuate this condition. He must see that the stage of development, which he has attained, is not lost and that he does not fall down from the height he has reached. This is the sixth stage of his flight.

After he has sufficiently persevered in his efforts, and has guarded the position for a sufficiently long period, he is to forget everything other than Him. He is to forget himself, the world, worldly things and all relations; in short he is to forget everything excepting the one idea of God.[1] This forgetfulness of everything besides Him is a symbol of perpetual bliss. This is abnegation of self in Him. It is the gate of Heaven, passport to merger in the Universal Divine Unity of Existence. It is to be remembered that this is the last stage to be achieved by a seeker.

According to another version there are seven stages or valleys which a seeker must pass through, before he merges into the Infinite. They are the preparatory stages, at each of which the seeker acquires a new character and after crossing them one after the other he draws nearer to his goal.[2] They are enumerated as follows[3]:—

1. Consciousness in breathing (Hūsh dar dam).
2. Carefulness in movement (Naẓar bar Qadam).
3. Movement in residence (Safar dar Waṭan).
4. Secrecy in society (Khalwat dar Anjuman).

---

1 Mujaddid Aḥmad Sirhindī: Letters, Vol. I. Letter 82.

2 *Ibid.* Letter 295.

3 Abul-'Alāī Faḍlu'd-dīn: Ḥaqīqatu'l-'Irfān, chap. on stages of the flight of spirit.

5. Perpetuity of consciousness (Diwām-i-āgāhī).
6. Criticism of consciousness (Muhāsabat-i-Nafs).
7. Permanence in annihilation (Baqā dar Fanā).

In the first stage the seeker must be conscious of the reality of God in every breath that he breathes. He should not pass a single moment of his life without being conscious of his relationship with the Infinite. Every occurrence, every activity, and everything that he attends to, should constantly remind him that he is a created being whose creator is Allāh, to Whom he owes his very being, and in Whom he lives.

When once he takes that attitude and begins to feel himself in the perpetual presence of God, he must necessarily begin to reform his actions and watch his movements. This is the second stage at which he not only begins to live in God, as at the previous stage but begins to act and move in Him, as well. The first stage consists in merely being aware of an Immortal Infinity while the second stage consists in acting according to the Infinite will. The first was merely the relationship of general awareness, while this is a definite relationship through the objective will. In the first stage the seeker was to take care not to breathe without the consciousness of the idea of God, and in this stage he is to be careful not to do any action without consciously relating it to the perpetual presence of God. At first he was merely to think according to the commands of God, and now he is to act for God, in obedience to God, in God and after God. I have already pointed out that the order of procedure, during the days of the supremacy of the Arab intellect, was different and opposite. Then a believer thought that he should begin by acting in obedience to and according to the law of God, and now a seeker always began by thinking of God first. But in a way this Sufi method was after the procedure of Islām which started with correcting the belief first and after the correction of ideas guided towards the right action.

Next the seeker is to detach himself from the association of place. He is to rise above the attachments of space and environment. He might live in a place, as physically he cannot but live in a place, but spiritually he must rise above place and its associations. He is to feel as if, while living in a place, he is constantly in travel. Living in a place or going away from it is not to affect his mind in the least. Space in mystic terminology represents the grossness of life, the material or vegetative element in human nature. Thus a seeker is not to attach any importance to place or to things that are in place. He is to dissociate himself from all that is material, spatial and worldly. God is immaterial, non-spatial and spiritual. In the spiritual progress, the material or non-spiritual element of life is to be totally neglected. This principle is equivalent to the principles of watching the number and watching the time in the previous scheme.

The next stage is retirement. It does not necessarily mean physical seclusion but mental retirement, concentration on the idea of the Beloved One, even when in society. At this stage the seeker is to rise above society. The attachment of persons, society, relatives and other associates is to be sacrificed for the attainment of the ideal. At previous stages he had to give up the associations of space, time and number, here he has to rise above his associations with other persons. In this spiritual progress he is to disregard the love of all his kith and kin. He is to sacrifice their affection for his love of God. This sacrifice is an essential stage in the attainment of His ideal. The heart must be purified and emptied of the love of all if God's love is to be realised.[1] One can live in retirement even while living in society.[2] It is a very desirable state of mental concentration. Learn to concentrate your mind upon your object of love in the presence of others. According to this view society is not necessarily inconsistent with the realisation of one's ideal, provided he does

---

1 Mark the following lines of Jāmī :

دارم دلی که باهر اندیشهٔ که داشت — جز یاد تو بر صفحهٔ خاطر نتگاشت

یاد تو چنان فرو گرفتش که درو — گنجائی هیچ چیز دیگر نگزاشت

Also a line from another Sufi poet:

ز یادِ غیر میگردد بدل یاد خدا کمتر — چو پرشد خانه می باشد بصاحبخانه جا کمتر

2 Mujaddid Aḥmad Sirhindī: Letters, Vol. II. Letter 38.

not attach any importance to it.

When the seeker has passed through all these stages, he will live perpetually with his Creator. He will think of Him and talk of Him alone. He will be perpetually busy with Him. He will never rest for a moment without Him.

The last stage is that of severe self-criticism. Here the seeker is to criticise his consciousness and to continue to examine it strictly in all its thoughts and feelings. He is not to allow any thought or action to pass uncriticised. This stage serves as a very valuable advice to all who advance towards a spiritual goal. It is a good advice even to those who have no ideals to attain, but intend to live a moral and happy life. If you can just weigh your actions and thoughts of the day before you go to sleep at night, it will provide you an excellent moral exercise and give you a very good moral training and teach you how to form right moral judgments. To repent for one's evil actions and to appreciate and feel pleasure in good ones before one forgets them is an excellent psychological method to improve one's practical morality. It checks you from persisting in the evil path and resists the tendency of the physical organism to repeat automatically its previous actions, and at the same time encourages you to do good and think aright.

This has been mentioned as the last stage, since the critical faculty is the last to be developed in the spiritual progress. The passing of correct spiritual judgments naturally comes as the last stage in the scientific theory of religious insight and spiritual flight. Moreover, criticism is useful and wholesome only when it comes after certain stages of progress. The misuse of this faculty is highly prejudicial to the spiritual progress. In early stages its use may prove more injurious than useful. But at a later stage it is highly beneficial and saves the seeker from many snares and pitfalls. It helps to distinguish right from wrong and good from evil. It is another name for conscience. I mean the faculty of criticism when applied to moral phenomena is called conscience. This stage is marked by development of a spiritual conscience in the seeker.

Every theory of stages or valleys ends with the seventh and the final stage of mystic experience, that is, Fanā, merger into the Infinite and the Absolute Reality, or Baqā, that is, perpetual living in Him. The theory of merger has already been dealt with in a previous chapter.

As for the classification of these various stages or valleys of spiritual progress it need not be pointed out that they are imaginary and any number of classifications can be mentioned. It is immaterial for a real seeker in how many parts or stages you divide or describe the flight of his spirit towards the Absolute Ideal and its abode of perpetual bliss. Properly speaking there are no stages. It flies and flies and every flight is marked with restlessness and anxiety to reach still nearer to its object of love and desire. The last stage of merger probably never comes, at least in this life, because after its achievement there would be no spiritual activity, which is simply equivalent to death. This theory of stages or valleys indicates as if there were so many halting places in the course of flight. No such conception is correct. It is a perpetual flight, without halts and without resting places. The Qur'ān says, "O man! surely you must strive hard (to attain) to your Lord, until you meet Him."[1] No such classification has been given by Islām. Its theory of the flight of spirit towards God is quite different. According to Islām, every action done according to His Law and in obedience to Him, and every thought about Him, leads the acting or the thinking creature unto Him.[2] After death all creatures retire unto Him. But even during their life, unquestioning and complete obedience to Him is the only way of their nearing to Him. The chief reason for the popularity of such un-Islāmic theories among the Sufis was the introduction of the authority of the Shaikh as coequal with that of the Qur'ān and Traditions. We shall now see what is the real Islāmic view about saintship.

---

1 The Qur'ān LXXXIV. 6.

2 Mujaddid Aḥmad Sirhindī : Letters, Vol. II. Letter 25.

CHAPTER VII.

SAINTSHIP IN ISLĀM AND ITS DECADENCE.

The grades of saintship as known among the Sufis at the present day were quite unknown to the founder of Islām or to his early followers. The Qur'ān, no doubt, had mentioned certain grades among the Muslims which could be achieved by every true believer if he could acquire certain attributes by faith and good actions. The grades in the order of spiritual piety and of nearness to God as mentioned in the Qur'ān are as follows:—(1) Prophets (Nabiyyūn), (2) Attestors (Ṣiddīqūn), (3) Martyrs (Shuhadā), (4) The Reformed (Ṣāliḥūn), (5) The Pious (Akhyār), (6) The Faithful (Mu'minūn), and (7) The Muslims (Muslimūn).[1] These are the seven ranks of piety among the Muslims, held by persons possessing certain attributes which characterise each class. From the Islāmic point of view these seven groups of people are sure to be saved from the fire of Hell and get salvation. It is very difficult to say definitely about any person, to which of these classes he belongs, excepting the prophets. But in certain cases the intuitive eye of a saint recognises the rank of another, and in the history of Islāmic Sufism there have been not a few

1 The Qur'ān IV, 69.

instances when one pious soul recognised the rank of another and accepted his lead. The Prophet is reported to have said, " One believer is the mirror for another." Out of a number of instances those of Maulānā Jalālu'd-dīn Rūmī who accepted Shams-i-Tabrīz as his Pīr, and Shiblī who recognised Junayd as his guide, may be quoted as having been well known to all. Some persons are believed to occupy one of these ranks by the consensus of opinion among the faithful. Abū Bakr, for instance, is said to be an attestor because the companions of the prophet unanimously recognised him as such. The class of prophets as opposed to others is unique and supreme in authority. A nation that failed to recognise its prophet was punished by Divine wrath and was overtaken by some calamity which ended its career on the earth.

The rank of the prophets is, therefore, the highest. They are a class of persons to whom God communicates His messages, His law, and His will in order to be propagated among the human beings, so that they may progress in this world and achieve salvation in the next, by acting according to them. They lead the human beings to Divinity by reforming their customs, habits, practices and beliefs. Their primary function of life is to glorify the name of Allāh.[1]

---

1 The Qur'ān XXI. 25.

The Qur'ān infers the necessity of raising the prophets among the children of Adam from the fact of possibility of human submission to the evil suggestions of Satan.[1] Since Adam had come to earth as the Vicar of God and Satan as a principle of evil, there arose the necessity of checking the evil and encouraging the good, a principle dominantly involved in Adam's creation. Thus the Qur'ān had shown that whenever in a particular land, or in the world at large, the evil principle was dominating over the real original nature of Adam, which was inherently good, a prophet was raised to re-establish the kingdom of God on earth to restore the dominance of the Divine element in human nature over the Satanic, to make the human nature what it really was, and to shake off the evils that crept into the human society on account of the temporary supremacy of Satan.

Lively, lengthy and complicated discussions are found in the writings of Muslim Theologians and Muslim Sufis whether the rank of prophethood is a sheer grace of Divine Will, or it is bestowed because of the possession of certain characteristics by a person to whom it is granted. The Qur'ān seems to hold that this spiritual rank is granted by Allāh merely out of His grace.[2] He raises to this rank whomsoever He chooses. In reply to the objections raised by the Jews that all the prophets

---

1 The Qur'ān II. 37-39.

2 *Ibid.* III. 72-73; also *ibid.* II. 105.

raised before Muḥammad were Israelites, the Qur'ān says that prophethood was purely an act of Divine discretion, and that it was not necessarily limited to any particular tribe or to the particular branch of a certain person. The prophets deliver the divine messages to humanity, so unless such a person has a spiritual access to the Divine Will, he is of no use for propagating and interpreting them.

On the other hand there are certain passages in the Qur'ān which suggest that God rewarded such and such for their good deeds by bestowing upon them the rank of prophethood.[1] Sufis, however, believe that a prophet, before he is raised to this rank, is a walī, which term means a lover or a friend of God, or one obedient to Him.[2] The Qur'ān says, "Verily the friends of Allāh shall have no fear, nor shall they grieve."[3] This view is not necessarily inconsistent with the former, as making a person walī also, according to the Sufis, depends solely upon the grace of Allāh.[4] Therefore it is immaterial whether a person is first given the rank of walī and then raised to the rank of prophethood, or whether he is directly raised to the higher rank, because in either case it is the pure grace of Allāh that counts.

---

1 The Qur'ān XXVIII. 62.

2 Lane: Lexicon, under Walī. 3 The Qur'ān X. 62.

4 Nicholson : Studies in Islāmic Mysticism. Abū Sa'īd's attitude towards this point, which he states while discussing the nature of Laṭīfa and Sin.

The school of Mu'tazilites believes that since God cannot do anything unreasonable, therefore, He is bound to raise to the rank of prophethood only those persons who bear an excellent character.

The view of Sufis appears to be more Islāmic than that of the Mu'tazilites. According to Islām, reason, as we conceive it, is not applicable to the Will of God, which is supreme to any conception of human reason. We possess different passions and instincts, and in order to make a choice among them we have to play one passion or instinct against the others, and the grounds on which we make our selection along with the process of inhibiting the rival instincts is called reason by us. But divine nature is free from such rival competition of instincts, since its unity completely excludes all plurality. We possess a plural nature, each element in which contends for superiority over all the rest. That is why for the continuation of the whole we sacrifice the special benefits of certain parts and choose a course beneficial to all. It is through the development of this kind of judgment of relative preference of one tendency over another, that reason comes to function in the tangle of our life. But does it mean that the idea of the unity of God in Islām involves the denial of the possibility of the existence of reason in Divine nature? It is in the human sense of the term that it is not applicable to the Divine Will. There may be grounds of choice for Him, and they may even relate to the ultimate good, or morality, but the ultimate motive of His decisions as in the case of human beings cannot be a desire to perpetuate His existence, as to Him there is no fear of the dissolution of different elements of His existence. Consequently there can be no limit or condition to His choice or action. In His case, therefore, there is no difference between acting and thinking. In Him to think is to do. The Qur'ān says, "His command, when He intends anything, is only to say to it, Be, and it becomes."[1] His will is free and there is nothing like history, previous ideas, or actions to bind it, as in our case. It is therefore more Islāmic to say that it wholly depends upon His will to select for His mission, whomsoever He chooses, but He causes such character to develop in him, even before selecting him for this purpose that he can be called a walī before he is chosen for prophethood.

Again, the Qur'ān tells us that there are different grades even among the prophets,[2] but it lays down a principle that Muslims should not consider any one of the class of prophets as inferior to others.[3]

There is no difficulty in reconciling the two views. According to the first view there is a difference of grades in the ranks of different prophets from the Divine standpoint, but the

---

1 The Qur'ān XXXVI. 82. 2 *Ibid.* II. 253.

3 *Ibid.* II. 285; and also III. 83.

followers of the prophet are not to differentiate among the members of this class to the discredit of any one. This injunction means that if prophets are to be regarded as Divine leaders of humanity they must be equally respected. Islām started with the preaching of love and affection towards the other communities, other religions, and their founders. It was founded on love, toleration and union and not on hatred and discord. It emphasised the elements of truth involved in other religions and tried to build its own structure on the material of those elements. The Sufis too tried to follow this principle. All movements that claimed to establish a universal religion, or a religion of humanity were nothing but so many less successful imitations of the original example set by Islām.

The Qur'ān lays down that every prophet in addition to the general mission of propagating the name and unity of Allāh, had a special sign given to him either in the form of a particular miracle or a special trait of character. For instance, it says about Moses, "And to Moses, Allāh addressed His words speaking (to him)."[1] Again it says about Job, "Surely We found him patient."[2] While the prophet Muḥammad is referred to in different contexts as possessing all the particular characteristics that were possessed by the other prophets

---

1 The Qur'ān IV. 164. 2 *Ibid.* XXXVIII. 44.

singly. If we study the Qur'ān minutely we shall arrive at the conclusion that each prophet represents a class of people, possessing certain attributes. Sometimes the Qur'ān leans towards dividing the prophets into two classes, one class comprising the prophet Muḥammad alone and the other class including all the rest of the prophets. The verse which refers to the covenant of the prophets and many others hint at such a classification.[1] The classification is not so absurd as it might look for putting only one person under one class. His personality is so great and so multiform that he by himself looks like a class.

But the real classification of the prophets, to which the Qur'ān clearly refers, is that which divides them into two classes, the prophets of firm determination and the rest.[2] Under the first category fall all those prophets who had to suffer a good deal at the hands of their opponents and oppressors, and who consequently had to show boundless courage, patience, and endurance under the persecutions, which they had to face. They had to work under very adverse circumstances, and in order to meet, defy and overcome the strong opposition they were granted a strong mind and an undaunted will. They worked hard and long, and were not discouraged by any kind of opposition, nor despaired of the ultimate triumph of their

---

1 The Qur'ān III. 80. 2 *Ibid.* LXVI. 35.

cause. Their persecuters were destroyed, their enemies were vanquished and their oppressors were laid low at their mercy. The prophets which are included in this category by the Qur'ān, are Noaḥ, Abraham, Moses, Jesus and the prophet Muḥammad, while all the rest fall under the second category.[1]

This classification is based only upon a difference of degree, upon the possession of more or less power of determination, persistence or constancy. But as a working classification, showing a difference in the richness of the contents of life of certain members of the general class of prophets, and as indicative of the degree of activity with which they fulfilled their mission, and the amount of opposition which they had to face, it is a valuable division.

" Prophets can be classified into two classes on another principle as well: those who were given a sacred book, in order that the influence of their teachings should continue after their life-time, and those who were not given any such book, and whose influence evidently, therefore, was intended to last during their life-time only."

This distinction is more sound than the previous one. Here one class is distinguished from the other on account of the possession of a certain attribute lacking in the other. The Qur'ān men-

1 The Qur'ān XXXIII. 7.

tions four such prophets: Moses who was given the Torah, David who was given the Zabūr, Jesus who was given the Injil or New Testament and Muḥammad who was given the complete Book—the Qur'ān. The Qur'ān also speaks of some scriptures having been given to Abraham.[1] This classification is evidently different from the previous one. The class of prophets with determination does not coincide with the class of possessors of a book, since the first contains Noaḥ and Abraham, who did not fall under the second, and excludes David, who falls under the second, the other prophets being common to both.

Another classification of prophets into two classes is possible. Those unto whom law was revealed and those to whom no law was revealed even though a book might have been revealed to them. The latter were bound to obey the law revealed to their predecessors. The prophets belonging to the previous class are called Law-givers while the others are called non-law-givers. On the basis of this principle only Moses and Muḥammad would belong to the first category and all the rest to the second. This principle of distinction is supported by the Qur'ān by likening Muḥammad to Moses. But this distinction is useful only if the term Law is to be understood in its modern usage of pure civil and criminal law.

1 The Qur'ān LXXXVII. 19.

But no prophet did really give law in this sense. The term Law as understood both by Moses and by Muḥammad had a wide implication, meaning a set or code of rules for the guidance of human beings for living well. It included not only juristic rules, but also spiritual, political, social, economical and most of all moral rules for the guidance of human conduct. In this wide sense of the term almost every prophet gave a set of rules to be acted upon by him who wanted to attain salvation. This distinction is, therefore, of very great value if we use the term Law in its wide sense.

Another distinction is sometimes made between apostles and prophets. The former are those who only propagate the message of Allāh, while the latter are those who give news about future, who foretell events along with the mission of propagating the Divine messages. But according to the Qur'ān the mission of all the apostles as a class is to warn people and to give them the good news.[1] Both these things relate to future events. It is difficult to say whether there has been any messenger who did not say anything about future. It is difficult to trace this distinction in the Qur'ān, which uses the two terms Rasūl and Nabī interchangeably.

For the first time in the history of religions, Islām had laid down that the prophets, though

1 The Qur'ān II. 213.

physically raised among different people in different lands, were the leaders of the whole human race. They had an extra-local or in other words a universal existence and therefore a universal claim to respect and honour from those who believed in one universal God, who had equal relations with all nations and all people. Islām had enjoined on the faithful to believe in the truth of the mission of all the prophets of the world, since it proceeded from a common source of the universal will of Allāh. Respect and believe the truth, wherever it may be, irrespective of its associations with time, age, space or locality. How far this article of Islāmic faith has helped to develop the modern scientific spirit, is not difficult to find. It was the practical application of this principle which was responsible, to a great extent, for such a rapid growth of scientific spirit among the early Muslims on account of which they could assimilate and build upon the Greek philosophy, Egyptian medicine and Roman law. It is on account of this article of faith that even today millions of Muslims claim the prophets and reformers of various nations as their own, so far as their real teachings are concerned. This principle was just becoming of a religion that claimed to be universal. It emphasised the uniformity of the mission of different prophets as much as it emphasised the unity of God. As a matter of fact one followed the other. If God was one, universal and unconditioned by place or time, then His message to humanity must also be one and uniform. Therefore, all the prophets had the same mission, that is, the fundamental principles in the teachings of all were almost the same, the difference being only in minute details which were adapted to the habits, customs and temperaments of different nations to which they were sent. This theory has been technically called, " The unity of Revelation."[1] It is based upon a fundamental principle of the unity of the purpose of revelation. We have seen that the prophets were sent to lead the people in their spiritual progress, to warn and caution them against the snares of Satan and against the punishment of hell fire. They were the spiritual leaders of humanity. Since, therefore, the cause of the advent of every prophet was the same, and since, moreover, they were sent by the same Eternal Personality and since human nature, though varying with different ages and localities yet involved certain constant, uniform and universal elements, the prophets must have had certain common and universal doctrines to preach, in whatever age or country they might have chanced to live. Briefly, the theory of the unity of Revelation is based upon more fundamental doctrines of the unity of God, community of the causes of the advent of prophets and the uniformity of human nature, at least in its spiritual

---

[1] وحدت رسالت

aspects.

From this principle of the unity of Revelation Ibnu'l-'Arabī evolved a science which he has discussed and elaborated in his famous book, "Fuṣūṣu'l-Ḥikam" "the Bezels of Divine Wisdom". Fuṣūṣ purports to be a treatise on the nature and attributes of God as manifested through the prophecy of different prophets, each of its 27 chapters dealing with the logos or Kalimah of a particular prophet as typifying and representing a particular Divine attribute. The theories set forth in the Fuṣūṣ are difficult to explain and not less difficult to understand. Often he takes a text of the Qur'ān and elicits his doctrines from it in a fashion peculiar to scholastic mystics.

It may be briefly summed up in this way. The Divine essence, which is all that exists, can be conceived in two different ways, either as a pure, simple, attributeless essence or as an essence endowed with attributes. God considered absolutely is beyond relation and consequently beyond knowledge. Al-Ghazāli thinks that God can be known without reference to the universe, but he seems to be mistaken. For while God is independent of created beings in respect of His essence, He requires them in relation to His Divinity. His existence is absolute, theirs is relative. Real Being becomes limited and individualised in appearing as a form of reality. Hence all things are attributes of God. As such they are identical with

God, apart from Whom they have no reality. To support this doctrine Ibnu'l-'Arabī has adduced arguments from the logos (kalimah) of every prophet. The special characteristics of every prophet are used by him to prove the essential unity of the One. The prophets in various countries and in different ages have been representing as so many attributes of the one Divinity; and this principle generalised is the substance of the whole treatise. It is clearly the theory of the unity of existence substantialised and based upon a definite line of thought and a definite scheme of reasoning.

Attestors.

The next class of saints according to Islām is that of the attestors (Siddīqūn). They are so called because they accept their prophet unquestioningly, and thus they are said to attest the Truth, that is, the prophet and his revelation, instinctively or intuitively. They are the first helpers of the prophet of their age. When an apostle is alone and forlorn, when his people mock at him and conspire against him, they are the first to come forward and help him and save him from the mockery of unbelievers and do not hesitate to sacrifice their life and property in their cause. They are the first to side with truth in its struggle against evil. Their hearts are fortified by faith while other people are steeped in sin.

Consequently as soon as the religion of the prophet, whose first supporters they were, gets established, they are the first to be venerated, worshipped or deified. As soon as the opponents of the prophets are vanquished, as they naturally must sooner or later, they are raised to a sublime position. It has been suggested, that their relation to their prophet is that of an echo with the real voice. They usually get a vague presentiment of whatever message is revealed to the prophet in clear words. There appears to be no exaggeration in the analogy. As these people are the first helpers and supporters of their prophets, they naturally get a fair knowledge of their tendencies, ideas, and views. When once the interests, thoughts, and views of two persons become identical, there is no ground for surprise if they think similarly about similar things under similar situations. Such is the case with attestors. Since they are the first to appreciate the truth, and help it actively, they are the first to get the reward and blessings for their good deeds.

So was Lot to Abraham, Aaron to Moses, the disciples to Jesus and the companions to Muḥammad of whom the chief was Abū Bakr. Innumerable traditions refer to their extreme devotion to their respective prophets. After the death of their respective prophets, sometimes even in their life-time they were the first to receive their reward, either in the form of being raised to prophethood, as in the case of Lot, Aaron and disciples of Jesus, or to the high dignity of Khilāfat as in the case of the companions of the prophet.

As they are the first to side with the truth they are the first to suffer persecution at the hands of their nation. Next to the prophets, they have to make the greatest sacrifices, and naturally, therefore, when the scales are turned, when the truth triumphs, as sooner or later it must, when the opposition is laid low, those people are the first to be rewarded and venerated.

According to some writers they also get a revelation, which is inferior in kind to that of the prophets. Whether they receive a revelation or not, it is at least quite certain that they think with the prophet, act like him and work with him to end the reign of sin and impiety and suffer with him in his struggles, and when the reign of impiety has ended they are usually the first to get their reward. Since they accept the truth of the Divine message unquestioningly, their moral and spiritual superiority over others is also recognised without any logic. They are readily accepted as the supreme authority in the matters of religion and piety and are recognised as the true successors of their prophet. They play the part of an interpreter between the prophet and his people. They bring out the meanings of the teachings and actions of the prophet by putting them in their practices.

The next class of saints according to the Qur'ān is that of the Martyrs. They are a class of believers, who seal the truth of their faith by their blood. They lay down their

Martyrs.

lives in the path of Allāh. They give the greatest practical proof of their faith. Their faith is not merely a lip devotion, but they prove by means of their actions, that their belief in the existence of God, and in the truth of the mission of the prophet is unshakable, firm and deep, and that no force on earth can change it and no power or fear can deflect it. Ordinarily the fear of death keeps us off from many a good and great deed, but there can be no limit to the spiritual progress of that soul which is prepared to lay down even its organism for the sake of Divine Love. No better proof can be given than this to prove the depth of one's devotion to his Beloved One.

The Arabic equivalent for the term martyr primarily means one who is a witness to a certain truth or fact.[1] It has come to mean a martyr because he is a witness to the faith in the existence of God and in the truth of the prophet's mission. According to the strict technology of Islām, a martyr is he who is killed, while struggling to bring about the supremacy of truth over falsehood, while acting only for the cause of Allāh. To act with any motive other than that of executing the command of God is not only not encouraged by Islām, but strictly prohibited. Therefore, a person who is killed while acting with any motive other than that would not be entitled to the high

1 شهيد comes from the same root as شاهد.

rank of a martyr. Islām had emphasised that in every age there should be a class of believers, who should invite people to good and enjoin what is right and forbid the wrong, and should carry on an unceasing struggle for the supremacy of truth.[1] The function of this class will be to keep peace in the world, to help the weak, to destroy the wrong and to dispel the darkness of sin. This class of the faithful should devote their time, energy and lives to the cause of Allāh alone, and should serve their faith, their fellow-beings and their nation. Their fellow-believers are bound to support them for their worldly necessities. This class is called by the name of "flock of Allāh".[2] The idea was similar to that of a class of Knights in the Middle Ages in the western world, with the only difference, which is of no small importance, that this devoted band of Muslims was to busy itself in establishing the supremacy of the name of Allāh, of the principles of good and not to wander from place to place in earch of romance, without any definite aim. This class of Muslims was intended to be an organised and disciplined society of volunteers with a definite programme of work, for achieving a definite object, while European Knights had neither this kind of discipline nor were they moved by such noble ideals.

There is no doubt that inspite of our extreme

1 The Qur'ān III. 103. 2 *Ibid.* LVIII. 22.

care and love for existence, which is implied in all our actions and thoughts, because the struggle for existence is a law of all biological phenomena, to lay down one's possessions in the cause of right and truth is the highest spiritual blessing to which any one can aspire. There is and always shall remain a class of such high-minded persons in the world as will not care a jot for their life whenever their honour is at stake, and their faith endangered. On such occasions, they attach no importance to their life. They think it to be in their best interest to lay it down quietly and ungrudgingly. Islām had attempted to organise such people and it is evident that after being organised they could achieve much better results. The reward promised to this class over and above that promised to the ordinary Muslims was that in return to their sacrifice of life they would never die. If a man gives away his temporary life for the sake of Allāh, Who is the source of all life, then He shall bestow upon him a perpetual, never-ending life, full of pleasure which can hardly be dreamt of in this existence on the globe.[1]

It is more or less a question of faith. All our activities in this life are directed towards the one object of living well. Every moment of our life

---

1 Rūmī : Mathnawī, Book 1 :

نان دهی از بهر حق نانت دهند　　جان دهی از بهر حق جانت دهند

Jāmī :

زان بس چو وجود یافت ازان مایهٔ ناز　　جاوید برو در عدم گشت فراز

is intended to be so spent as to contribute something to our future welfare. Martyrdom, that is, readiness to lay down one's life in the path of Allāh, appears the shortest cut to the blessings of perpetual life. If a man can believe that Allāh's promises must be fulfilled, then the shortest cut to His perpetual bliss appears to be to lay down one's life unhesitatingly in His path.[1] It was this faith in the fulfilment of the promises of Allāh that made the early Muslims fight in the battle-fields so fearlessly. It is this preparedness to lay down one's life in the cause of truth by which you can always judge and measure the degree of awakening and spiritual progress in any nation.

There has been a good deal of discussion as to the nature of this eternal life which has been promised to the martyrs as a reward for the sacrifice of their lives in the cause of truth. One school is of opinion that their lives and deeds are perpetuated in the minds of the contemporary and future generations of the nation to which they belong. Since they sacrifice their life for the cause of their nation their people in return perpetuate their memory through legends, literature and history. But this explanation appears to be far-fetched and does not justify the strong language of the Qur'ānic text. People do not usually perpetuate the memory of every martyr. For a short time their memory

1 The Qur'ān XXXIX. 20.

might keep fresh, but after that time it is sure to be obliterated by the liveliness of contemporary events. Again, the ideas of right and wrong might change in nations and a martyr to-day might become a horrible traitor to-morrow. A warm appreciation through sympathetic feelings for the sufferings of a person, when looked at to-morrow through the cold rational perspective of past historical records might make us pass a different judgment altogether. The appreciation of the masses for any deed does not really show that the deed is virtuous. Even the contemporaries of a person may hold different and sometimes contradictory opinions about him. The reason is obvious. Everybody judges the deeds of others, sometimes even his own, in the light of his personal views of right and wrong. Therefore, in spite of the fact that we all agree in theory that there is some such thing as a universal ethical standard, in actual practice we find that two persons watching a certain deed at the same time and from the same place, give different judgments and sometimes inconsistent ones about the ethical merits of that deed. Thus if no two persons even among the contemporaries can agree on the merits of the sacrificial deed of a person then it is no reward for him to be given a perpetual life which may not live in the memory of any living person, and which even if appreciated by a few may not last longer than a few generations.

Take an example from among the mystics themselves. Manṣur al-Ḥallāj is credited with being the head of martyrs by a section of Sufis, while a large number of Muslims consider him only to be an unbeliever (Zindīq).[1] If this is really the meaning of perpetual existence, then it is only far-fetched and unreliable and can never be a sufficient motive for laying down one's life.

Moreover, to call the conceptual notion of a thing as real existence is an Aryan idea. According to Aryan philosophy things possess two kinds of existence, one conceptual, so far as it is a part of the world of ideas, and the other material, so far as it is a part of the tangible and sensible universe. But the Semitic mind was too practical to conceive the universe of abstract ideas as real in any sense. The fact is amply illustrated by the difference between the Semitic conception of one God and the latter development of the Sufi doctrine of Abstract Unity of Existence, which was due to the influence of the literature and philosophy of Aryan races. So this interpretation of the verse seems to have a touch of Aryan philosophy. On the other hand, the perpetual life promised by the Qur'ān seems to be a life somehow or other related to the real and tangible existence.

The Qur'ān has never used the term "life" in

---

1 Nicholson: Studies in Islāmic Mysticism, p. 32, where Abū Sa'īd's attitude towards Manṣur's death is given; cf. Browne: Literary History of Persia, p. 423, for discussion of the opposite view.

the mere conceptual sense. Whenever the term is used in the Qur'ān, whether with reference to the theory of Resurrection or in any other context, it always implies some kind of consciousness with a certain tangible body, however ethereal that body might be, but something other than a mere thought, a mere idea, an image or a fancy of mind.

Again, this perpetuation in the form of national memory may appeal to a modern mind for whom there can be no higher motive than national cause for self-sacrifice, but the kind of martyrdom which Islām demands is of a much higher type. It is to lay down one's life for the sake of Allāh, and in the cause of truth. Such a sentiment and faith cannot adequately be rewarded by the continuation of existence merely as a thought in the mind of the nation. Islām emphasises obedience and love of God as the chief motives of action. A sacrifice in obedience to Him, and for His love, must, therefore, be rewarded in the terms of His pleasure, His approval and His kindness.

Sufis accordingly understand by the perpetuity of the life of a martyr a sort of merger into God. The general doctrine of merger has already been examined in detail in a previous chapter, where we arrived at the conclusion that Islām does not countenance the view that the created beings can ever become merged into the Creator. The very idea of the merger of one thing into another involves that both the things possess some kind of physiological contents which can be spatially related. It is possible to conceive that human soul, on account of its inseparable connection with the physical organism, may have some such content, but this conception cannot be applicable to God, by any stretch of imagination, unless He is conceived in a grossly material way. Therefore, whether you conceive the soul immaterial like God, or unlike Him, the analogy is not applicable. In the first case, their combining together will have a unique form which cannot be described or conceived in the terms of spatial relations, and thus something indescribable and inconceivable, while in the second it will be a fusion of two unlike things having nothing in common which may serve as the medium of combination.

It was on this basis that Islām had created an impassable channel between the Creator and the created. Anything might change into another, but a created being was separated from the Creator by such hard and fast lines as could never be crossed. The idea of Creator as preached by Islām was so sublime, so unique and pure, that no jugglery of words could possibly make the created ones equal to the Creator. If there was no possibility of equality, then there was no possibility of merger, for then it would mean even greater degradation for the Supreme Creator. The merger theory, as I have pointed out above, is also coloured with a tinge of the Indian theory of Absolute soul or Brahma.

Moreover, when one's personality merges into another it ceases to live. To call this state a life eternal or otherwise is a misnomer and is to do violence to the meaning of the term 'life'. It is apparent from the text quoted above that the life promised to a martyr by the Qur'ān is not a life like that of God, firstly because martyrs are mentioned as being given food and drink, the want of which has been denied to God, and secondly because the existence of God has been established by the Qur'ān as an easy thing to be grasped, while about them it is said that one cannot understand what kind of life they enjoy. It is quite evident, therefore, that the Sufi interpretation of the perpetual existence of the martyr as merger into God is neither quite sound nor quite in consonance with the basic principles of Islām.

The third interpretation given is that they live with their bodies like ourselves, only that they are hidden from our senses, which not being keen enough, cannot feel their existence. It is the most material interpretation of the perpetual life promised to them. But if so is the case, why can we not understand their existence? When the Qur'ān offered the theory of resurrection of bodies after death, when we can understand the existence of minute microscopic creatures which cannot be perceived by means of naked senses, there is no reason why it should have been declared in such categorical terms in the Qur'ān that human intellect was unable to comprehend the life led by the martyrs.

It has been pointed out by others that this existence is purely spiritual, the food and drink which they get are as well spiritual, being nothing but the nearness, kindness and mercy of God. From the point of view of this explanation the different stories generally found in the inferior kind of Sufi literature and related by the ignorant and the credulous, viz., those of seeing the martyrs, of talking with them, and praying to them and of their prayers having been granted, would come to be nothing more than mythological rubbish, an allegorical way of describing the spiritual elevation of their soul.

To cut the discussion short, we may say that they live a kind of life which, according to the Qur'ān, is difficult, nay impossible for us to grasp. One thing is certain that their life is neither like that of God, nor like that of ours, since we can conceive both of them without much difficulty. It is a peculiar kind of existence granted to them in lieu of the temporary life which they have sacrificed. In any case it must be better than the temporal life which they have given up, inasmuch as the very idea of reward implies that it must be better than that for which it is a reward. Their memory is worthy of veneration, since they have laid down their highest possession for the sake of their Beloved. They have set an example of self-sacrifice which must be followed by every one who wants to attain to spiritual height. They have given evidence of their faith by means of their blood, each drop of which shall speak for them on the Day of Judgment when the deeds shall be reckoned, and the final judgment delivered. Every drop of their blood shall be a witness to their heart-felt love for God. Islām has encouraged martyrdom, by raising the martyrs to a peculiar kind of saintship which consists of perpetual life and everlasting bliss.

The Reformed (Ṣāliḥūn) and the Pious (Akhyār).

They are a class of persons who regulate their life and habits in accordance with the law of the Qur'ān. They instinctively obey God, and follow the prophet. They are the chosen ones among the faithful, and their merit is wholly dependent upon their good actions and their sound belief. Whenever they are called upon to do a thing, they do it without the least grudge, and when they are prohibited from doing a thing they would desist from it at once. They live like the ordinary people of the world, but their worldly cares, their likes and dislikes, their desires and wishes are regulated by the Law. They do not perform any extraordinarily meritorious deeds, but their actions and movements are controlled by certain principles, and by certain rules of life. There is a certain uniformity and consistency in their thoughts and actions, which comes from the respect which they have for the Apostle of Allāh, and his mission.

They form a class of moderately good Muslims. They are neither venerated nor worshipped, excepting perhaps in rare cases, but they are a source of peace and comfort to the people around them so long as they live, and are remembered, with affection and respect after their death by those who had had an occasion of dealing with them during their life. Within a limited circle of friends and acquaintances they are always regarded as the charm of society. They are innocent creatures, and would not harm any one except inadvertently in good faith. They are honest, reliable, fair in all their dealings with others. They are careful to fulfil their vows and promises. They possess all the natural capacities but only use them moderately. They perform the ordinary duties enjoined by Islām with utmost care and rigidity. They offer their prayers, fast during the month of Ramaḍān, pay the poor-rate regularly, and go to Mecca for pilgrimage if their means allow. They speak to their neighbours gently, treat their friends kindly, help the poor, relieve the needy whenever they can. In short, they are the type of persons that Islām intended to create out of the rough human material.

Islām has distinguished the class of the faithful or believers from that of the Muslims. By the faithful is meant a class of Muslims who have realised in their hearts what they profess with their tongues.[1] They attest with their hearts what they utter with their tongue, although for entering into the pale of Islām, only the utterance of a few set words is all that is required.

The Faithful or Believers (Mu'minūn); Muslims (Muslimūn).

So far as human beings are concerned it makes no difference whether the person, who is uttering the set words which entitle him to enter into the pale of Islām, is indeed a believer at heart or is simply an impostor and a liar. But the all-knowing and the all-seeing God, from Whom no mysteries are hidden will reward or punish them according to their innermost thoughts. Thus mere lip professions of faith might deceive us who cannot penetrate beyond the mere surface of things, but they cannot deceive God. The faithful were never regarded as a class of saints by Muslims, since every Muslim was expected to be a believer also. Therefore no special importance was ever accorded to them as a class of saints, although, in reality, Islām expected every Muslim to become as pious as a saint.

---

1 The Qur'ān XLIX. 14.

This briefly was the Qur'ānic classification of saints in the order of their nearness to God. But the Sufis have developed a different classification of saints. According to them there are four classes of saints: Aqṭāb (Poles), A'immah (Leaders), Autād (Pegs) and Abdāl (Substitutes), who are also called Rijālu'l-Ghaib (mysterious ones).

Sufi theory of Saintship.

There is only one Quṭb who rules the universe at a time. When he vacates his seat, another of the same rank takes his charge. His duty is to execute the commands of God in the universe directly or through the instrumentality of an Imām, Autād, or Abdāl. There are two Imāms who rule the hidden and the visible worlds, one of them being in charge of each. They obey the commands of the Quṭb, who directly orders them to do things as he wants them to be done, according to the orders and wishes of God. They can directly communicate with Allāh, but ordinarily they execute His orders as received through the Quṭb.

Then there are the four Autād, each one to take care of the four sides, north, south, east and west. They are subordinate to the commands of both Quṭb and Imām. Then there are the seven Abdāl or Rijālu'l-Ghaib, one for each clime. They execute those commands of Allāh that they receive through the Quṭb and the Imām. The Quṭb is the superiormost and looks after all the various kinds of saints.

Whenever any one of the saints leaves his place by death or otherwise, the vacancy is filled up by the person next in rank. There is no direct recruitment, the highest rank can only be attained by patiently passing through all the slow degrees of promotion. They keep peace in the world and save it from calamities.[1]

The theory, briefly speaking, conveys the notion of the government of God in the universe through His chosen ones, a form of spiritual hierarchy. The idea underlying this classification appears to be something like this. This world is full of evil and evil persons. But evil without an admixture of good is pure negation and would mean chaos and destruction; therefore God governs the world through the principle of good and virtue, which does not exist in abstract but is concretely possessed by some created human beings. Those persons in whom this principle of good is incorporated are saints through whom He maintains peace in the universe and keeps it agoing. Among the saints there are

1 This theory is given in detail in Ibnu'l-'Arabi's famous book Futūḥātu'l-Makkiyyah, chapters 73 and 383, the last one being particularly devoted to the discussion of this theory. Ash-Sha'rānī has also dealt with this theory in great detail.

This theory is differently stated by Jāmī in Nafaḥātu'l-Uns (Calcutta Ed. 1858), p. 21. According to Jāmī's view there are in all 4000 saints who do not know one another. Out of them 300 know one another and consult each other. They are called Akhyār. Besides them there are 40 Abdāl, 7 Aḥrār, 4 Autād, 3 Nuqabā and one Quṭb or Ghauth. I have taken Ibnu'l-'Arabī's theory as representative of the Sufi view. All are equally arbitrary and imaginary.

different grades. Some of them are higher in rank and nearer to God than others and can directly communicate with Him. It is to be remembered that God not only executes His spiritual orders through them, but even in the execution of secular affairs they have a great hand. Hence the popular belief and practice of beseeching the saints to intercede for them before God, for their spiritual as well as worldly welfare.

Islām never contemplated any such classification of saints. Islām indeed attempted to bring about a government of saintly beings, a Theocracy, but not in the sense implied in this theory. Islām had pressed that none excepting those who were believers in One God and His prophets, deserved to rule and govern the world, because it was only in this way that peace could be maintained in the world. There is no doubt that the personality of the governors plays an important part in developing the character of the ruled But this benefit cannot possibly accrue in the case of a government by saints, as contemplated by this theory, because according to this view the saints need not necessarily reveal their rank to the masses nor need they have a political superiority as conceived by Islāmic view of Theocracy.

This theory smacks of the activities of 'Abdu'l-lāh b. Maymūn and Ḥasan b. Sabbāḥ, and other groups of reactionaries, who had two kinds of missionaries amongst them, known and hidden.[1] The leaders who are in charge of the outer and inner worlds and who are called Umanā' (Honest) by certain writers, perhaps represent this scheme of two kinds of missionaries. The theory of Seveners by Baṭinites may explain the rank of seven Abdāl, while some jurisconsults of the highest rank had recognised the necessity of two Imāms in the sense of theocratic rulers for the Muslim world.[2] It is not unlikely that these groups of reactionaries borrowed this idea of government of the world by saints from Plato's Republic. It contemplated to create an ideal state governed by the philosophers, who were transformed into saints under the influence of the Islāmic view of theocratic government. Islām was conscious of the fact that the world was not so ideal as Plato's Republic implied. It also knew that if the principle of good constantly predominated over that of evil, the conception of the next world could be safely dispensed with. Islām had impressed the need of resurrection, and of a Day of Judgment, because good men are not always rewarded nor evil always punished in this life. So this mystic theory involves a false premise that the government of the world is carried only by the principle of good. It is not so, for sometimes even evil may get the upper hand though it may be only temporary.

---

1 O'Leary : Arabic Thought, p. 195.

2 Macdonald : pp. 40, 41, 46.

Again, the number of saints fixed in each class is simply arbitrary and imaginary, unless it had some secret relation to the rank and numbers of missionaries of some one of the reactionary groups already mentioned.

This theory is clearly a development of those days when saints had begun to be worshipped as intermediaries to God. But this theory goes a step further than the theory of intercession. The latter only placed intercessors between men and God to plead for men, but this theory placed saints also as executors of God's will which was recognised by almost every religion to be directly operative, without the intermediacy of any persons. Even messengers did not claim to wield any divine power, while this theory invested certain saints with the divine power which they could exercise for the benefit or harm of human beings.

Thus, this theory is a complete departure from all that is Islāmic, and is believed to explain the influence Sufis have, the power that they can wield, for the advantage or disadvantage of others. That simple principle of praying to God was almost forgotten, and the revelation through the prophet of Islām ceased to have much value for a Sufi as every one could have it direct from God.

It may be asked why at this stage of the development of the Sufi doctrines so much importance was being attached to such imaginary and unreal classifications of the saints? The position becomes quite clear to us when we understand that it is a period of general degeneration in the Islāmic world. Its distinguishing feature is the popular and practical acceptance of the theory of intercession of persons for the attainment of salvation. The personality of the Shaikh or the spiritual leader looms large. The spiritual leader can pray for his followers, can ask blessings from Allāh on their behalf, and can remove their spiritual or worldly troubles. He can even take the responsibility of getting the sins of his followers forgiven. In some cases he even guarantees their salvation and promises their safe entry into the garden of Allāh, in return of a paltry sum to be paid to him for the services.

It is an age of saint-worship in the literal sense of the word. Every city of moderate size has its own patron saint. Even villages of very small dimensions have their own patron, while big cities have more than one, who claim to divide the city among themselves.[1]

The matter did not end here. The dead saints began to be worshipped. They began to be considered as intercessors on behalf of their followers before God and even sacrifices were offered on their

---

1 For more information, *vide* Brown: Dervishes, Chap. III.

tombs. Their aid was invoked, under the belief that they heard and granted their payers.[1] They were actually seen in dream or in wakefulness by their pious followers, specially by those who claimed to be their successors either by blood or by spiritual relationship. They were said to guide their followers or worshippers sometimes invisibly through spiritual media and sometimes by visiting them in person.

It is quite clear from this how far the Aryan, more particularly Persian, element had influenced the mind of the Muslim public. Islāmic traditions were being modified by the Persian legends. The ancient traditions of Persia were assiduously sought out and revived into practice. Literature became full of them and the public mind was greatly influenced by them. The Semite common sense was overpowered by the theoretical Aryan philosophy of Persian and Greek origin. The result was an indefinite and vague hotch-potch, one aspect of which was mysticism in the form which it had now adopted. Christian element was getting stronger through its influence upon the Caliph's court. Christians were becoming prominent as translators of the works on philosophy in the Arabic language. Their influence was responsible for saint-worship and for the popularisation of the theory of intercession

---

1 Nicholson : Studies in Islāmic Mysticism, p. 24. The attitude of Sufis like Abū Sa'īd towards the visitation of the tombs of saints to receive blessings from the spirits of the buried saints is represented here. There is great mystic literature on the point.

of persons to a great extent. For fear of the strong section of orthodox Muslims the mischievous doctrines could not be preached openly. Therefore, the method adopted to bring about the desired object was to give their theories a garb of religion and describe them in the Islāmic terminology,[1] though later on when the strong grip of the orthodox Islām became looser even this garb was dropped off and the terminology was openly changed. No doubt this was a roundabout way, but it was certainly the surest way of achieving the object. Had they openly revolted against the orthodox principles of Islām in the very beginning, the movement, in all probability, would have been put down with severity.

The circumstances that favoured the successful propagation of such theories were the advent of Greek philosophy in the courts of Arab rulers, who were now slowly yielding to Persian influences, the civil wars among the various sects and various dynasties for political supremacy, and above all the weakening of the influence of the early Islāmic traditions among the Muslim public.

The conditions described in this chapter continue to exist even up to the present day. Many reformatory movements among the Muslims have begun and ended without affecting the mind of the Sufis in the least. Wahhābī-ism in India and in Najd, Bahā'ī-ism in Persia, Aḥmadī-ism in India and Sanūsī-ism in Africa are some of them. So far as

---

1 Nicholson: Literary History of the Arabs, p. 392.

Sufism is concerned the first and the last only are relevant. The first was started as a protest against all that was unorthodox, un-Islāmic and contrary to the Book or the Sunnah.[1] It was a general reform movement for the whole of the Muslim community. It simply disbelieved that Sufism was an Islāmic theory or that it was a true representation of the faith. It was a direct challenge to Sufism. It held the Sufis responsible for a number of polytheistic practices that had become prevalent among the credulous Muslims as religious duties. It made an effort to re-establish Islām on the basis of its original traditions as handed down by the prophet and his early followers. It particularly attacked and condemned saint-worship, tomb-worship and the association of certain divine attributes with saints, as those things were considered responsible for introducing polytheistic beliefs and tendencies among the Muslims who as a community were believers in a sublime kind of pure Theism.[2]

The reaction of the Sufis against this movement was not long to be waited for. Ibn Taymiyah, whose works were responsible for this movement, was persecuted and imprisoned. Sufis as a class were the first to get offended by the principles of this reformation. They were foremost in condemning it, and probably rightly so, out of the sheer instinct of self-preservation. Sufism has borrowed

---

1 Macdonald : Theology, p. 60.

2 *Ibid.* p. 284.

so much from un-Islāmic sources that any movement which aims to establish the original purity and simplicity of Islāmic religion is sure to be opposed and condemned by Sufis as a class. Its reactionary attitude towards Wahhābī-ism was not, therefore, unnatural or unexpected.

For a very long time the Turkish government, merely out of political fears, continued to suppress the espousers of this movement. The Christian powers also helped the Turkish government to crush it. It was a menace to any government that ruled any number, however small, of the Muslims. A reformed orthodox Muslim would grow to be a political menace to any government, and this truth was clearly understood by all those governments which governed Muslims. Political suppression, therefore, from all directions kept this movement in the back-ground for a very long time and did not allow it to work itself out to its logical length.

Moreover, this movement like all others slowly degenerated into formalism which is highly destructive for any reformatory movement. Every new movement in order to succeed must make an allowance for free thought, and freedom of opinion and leave a sufficiently wide scope for variation in the ceremonials enjoined by it as was freely done by Islām. But this movement began to emphasise the formal rigidity which naturally weakened the zeal of its espousers. The result was that it failed to strike at the root of the weaknesses which it had undertaken to eradicate. Again with the zeal of its present head Ibn Sa'ūd, who is now master of whole Arabia, it is regaining its original vigour and now it appears to be only a question of time for it to eradicate the degenerated Sufism out of the Muslim world.

A similar movement of reformation was started in India by Mujaddid Aḥmad of Sirhind, and culminated in the writings of Shāh Walī'ullāh of Delhi. An attempt was made by Sayyid Aḥmad of Bareilly, who belonged to this school of thought, to reconquer India with the help of the frontier people, but he could not succeed. The reasons of his failure were many, but it will serve no useful purpose to discuss them here. It may be remembered, however, that although this movement was started on lines similar to that of Ibn Taymiyah, it was not an open attack on Sufi practices. This movement conceded mysticism to be Islāmic in nature and attempted to reform it like other Islāmic institutions. It attempted to purify Islām as well as Sufism of all its unnatural growths. The method followed for the re-establishment of the pristine simplicity of Islām was to offer the Qur'ān and the Traditions of the prophet as the only standards of faith and action. This movement like Wahhābī-ism in Arabia is gathering momentum in the activities of Ahlu'l-Ḥadīth.

Another movement which was more directly

connected with the reformation of Sufism was Sanūsī-ism in Africa. It was a reformation within the pale of Sufism. Its founder was himself a renowned Sufi and intended to reform Sufis on their own grounds, and according to their own principles. So far as the general reformation of the Muslims is concerned, both these movements were based upon almost the same principles. The object of both was to reform the Islāmic society on the basis of original Islāmic traditions, and to check its growing tendency in the direction of polytheistic practices. Both aimed at bringing about the original simplicity and purity of life in the society. Both of them attached due importance to the principles of holy war and Tablīgh or propagation of the faith, which were being totally neglected by the Muslims.

Sanūsī-ism no less than Wahhābī-ism was a menace and a danger to those governments that ruled Muslims. It was therefore persecuted by the European powers no less than the other, which having originated in Arabia first attracted the attention of the Turkish government and of the European powers only indirectly. Sanūsī-ism, on the other hand, having originated in Africa threatened the European policy of conquest and expansion on that continent more directly, and consequently unlike Wahhābī-ism was an object of a direct attack by European powers. Sanūsī-ism differs from its sister movement, in so far as it refers to Sufism directly, while the other only refers to it indirectly. Wahhābī-ism refuses to accept it as a true representation of Islām, while Sanūsī-ism believes Sufism to be a valid representation of Islām, provided it is reformed in certain respects. The founder of this movement and his successors are called Shaikhs or spiritual guides. Sanūsī-ism is more akin to the Indian movement of reformation started by Aḥmad Mujaddid of Sirhind and supported by Walī'ullāh of Delhi. This movement, although harried out of Africa by the high-handedness of the Italian government, is still gaining ground among the Arabs.

There is one distinguishing feature of all Sufi movements that they are considered as a source of danger by the government of the country in which they originate. This feature, though usually associated with Sufi movements since the days of the Assassins, is not really of great importance. But the heated imagination of a politician finds a political danger in every movement though it may be purely of religious or social nature. The existing European governments are particularly sensitive to the reformatory movements among the Muslims. Call a movement political and the rulers get a justification for suppressing it and massacring its espousers. It seems the modern capital-ridden governments are afraid of the reformed Islām which is socialistic in its principles and tendencies, and therefore constitutes a menace to all governments based upon blind individualistic capitalism, whether they may be bureaucracies or so-called democracies. But Islām never distinguished the political aspect of a movement from its theological, spiritual and social aspects. Islām itself was an all-embracing movement, which in abstraction could be analysed into so many aspects, but which in reality was concretely one and unanalysable, and so it had no clearly defined parts with clearly defined boundaries. Every living movement like a living organism is an active expansion in multifarious directions. Life is one single movement onward, not in one direction but in innumerable branches. Abstract analysis may give this branch or that branch more prominence but the concrete onward march of life is one and single act indistinguishable in parts so long as it lasts. The same was the case with Islām and same is the case with all Islāmic movements which take their origin from that living source. Every Islāmic movement, therefore, in whatever country and under whatever circumstances it may rise, must possess a political aspect as well as theological, spiritual, social, legal and various others, inseparably intermingled with one another. Islām does not attach primary importance to the political aspect, but the imagination of modern politicians, having been taught to attach the highest value to it, looks only to this aspect of such movements.

We may now briefly sum up our discussion and say that the various reformatory movements started in the Islāmic world have not yet proved of any great value. The pernicious practices introduced in the circle of their credulous votaries by the illiterate Sufis still persist and are considered to be the essence of Sufism, by some still more ignorant to be the essence of Islām. The time is ripe for reformation. Sufis as a class are no more than parasites living upon the income of Muslims. The Shaikhs get a fixed share of the income of their disciples and live a luxurious life, sometimes even more luxurious than the rulers of big states.

But there have always been noble exceptions, not wanting even in our own days. Some of the Shaikhs even now are of a high moral character, of great service to society and of real saintly nature. They work for their own livelihood and act according to the dictates of the Qur'ān and Traditions. They are extremely honest in all their dealings and sincere in their faith. In their silence and serenity they shed their light and lustre all around them and are a source of spiritual pleasure and elevation for all those who come in contact with them. But for these few, Islām should have been a dead religion. It should be remembered, however, that they have achieved all this not by following the mystic practices of the so-called Sufi writers, but by a simple childlike faith in God as Creator, Muḥammad as His last apostle and the best guide, and the Qur'ān as the last and most complete message of God to humanity.

INDEX OF PROPER NAMES.